BAPTIMERGENT

BAPTIST STORIES FROM THE EMERGENT FRONTIER

Smyth & Helwys Publishing, Inc.
6316 Peake Road
Macon, Georgia 31210-3960
1-800-747-3016
©2010 by Smyth & Helwys Publishing
All rights reserved.
Printed in the United States of America.

The paper used in this publication meets the minimum requirements of
American National Standard for Information Sciences—
Permanence of Paper for Printed Library Materials.
ANSI Z39.48–1984. (alk. paper)

Library of Congress Cataloging-in-Publication Data

Baptimergent: Baptist Stories from the Emergent Frontier / Zach T. Roberts, editor.

p. cm. Includes bibliographical references and index.
ISBN 978-1-57312-551-2 (pbk. : alk. paper)
1. Baptists—United States—Biography.
2. Emerging church movement—United States.
I. Roberts, Zach T. BX6493.B35 2009 286.092'273—dc22 [B] 2009047932

BAPTIMERGENT

BAPTIST STORIES FROM THE EMERGENT FRONTIER

ZACH ROBERTS, EDITOR

PRAISE FOR BAPTIMERGENT: BAPTIST STORIES FROM THE EMERGENT FRONTIER

Baptists—Southern, American, South American, Australian, Kiwi, Canadian, European, etc.—have played a quiet but pivotal role in the emergent conversation since the beginning. Meanwhile, some of their fellow Baptists have positioned themselves as outspoken antagonists of all things emergent. That's one reason this collection of essays is so important: it makes clear that in spite of a vocal opposition, there is also a growing chorus of creative and constructive Baptimergent voices. The uninformed, the opposed, the interested, and the already-involved will all find a rich combination of education, inspiration, provocation, and stimulation in these pages.

—*Brian D. McLaren*
Author, A New Kind of Christianity

The time has come for particular confessional tribes within Christianity to reflect on what the burgeoning emergence of the church means to them. *Baptimergent* is an excellent model of what that reflection can be—plus it has chapters by some of my favorite people in the world. This is a great resource for Baptists and non-Baptists.

—*Tony Jones*
Author, The New Christians: Dispatches from the Emergent Frontier

This collection of *Baptist Stories from the Emergent Frontier* is not only passionate and informing, but also precedent-setting. For the first time, emergence Christian leaders from a single faith tradition within Christianity have turned and, in love, affection, and devotion, addressed their denomination itself about who and what they are as dwellers within the dual context of emergence Christianity and a denominational loyalty. What they have to say matters to all of us.

—*Phyllis Tickle*
Author, The Great Emergence

In memory of Dr. Stuart McGehee,
whose passion for history inspired my reverence for the human story

To Dr. H. Leon McBeth,
whose prophetic storytelling inspired the same in me

ACKNOWLEDGMENTS

This project would not have been possible without the stories of those who wrote each chapter. I am grateful to them, and to the spirit of emergence that has allowed our paths to cross—physically and virtually.

I am deeply indebted to Keith Gammons for being open to this project and blessing it, and to Leslie Andres for covering up my weak editing skills and cracking the whip. Your patience and guidance are much appreciated. Thanks also to Smyth & Helwys for being willing to stretch the discourse on being Baptist.

To emergent facilitators like Brian McLaren, Tony Jones, Doug Paggit, Tim Conder, and Phyllis Tickle, I am deeply grateful for your conversations, insight, and listening ears. It is good to call you friends.

I am also grateful to those Baptist voices not represented in this book. To mentors, ministers, and colleagues like Ken Massey, Steve Presley, George Fuller Jr., Ken Myers, Velma Ferrell, Beverly Hatcher, Linda Jones, Chris Copeland, Brian Ammons, Bill Leonard, Steven Fuller, Chad Reed, and Rick Trexler. Thanks for being truth tellers, guides, brain-pickers, critics, and most of all, friends.

Finally, thank you, Jenn, Landyn, and Harrison. While I have struggled to find a "homeplace" for the way I understand my faith, my home is always with you. For that I am most grateful.

CONTENTS

INTRODUCTION

EMERGENCE IS NATURAL

When we discuss emergence, we are *not* dealing with a battle. The culture of the Western church has been engaged in ideological warfare for so long that it is hard to imagine that the emergent movement is not more of the same. Would it scare you if we said the emergent movement is an evolutionary necessity? Maybe the colloquialism that argues, "Where man puts a period, God puts a comma," would go over better.

Christian emergence is the insatiable pursuit of transcendent mystery. We have not captured God with our concepts, theologies, and creeds. There will always be more of God to discover.

The emergent movement is not an ideological alternative to "church-as-it-has-always-been." On the contrary, emergence is what happens within any living system. Emergence is an organic happenstance. If it tells us anything, it tells us that though some elements of the church may be dying, new life is also emerging in the present.

The term "emergent" as applied to the latest movement within Western Christianity is borrowed from biology, specifically fields relating to horticulture (plants) and arboriculture (trees). When scientists want to judge the health of a forest or "stand," one of the tools they employ is a ground survey. Part of a ground survey involves getting on hands and knees and evaluating the emerging growth on the forest floor. The emerging growth helps convey the status of a forest ecosystem. It is a key indicator in a complex matrix of organic occurrences that helps scientists relate and respond to a given ecosystem.

The Christian conversation-turned-movement now labeled "emergent" tells the church something about the overall Christian ecosystem in Western culture. The emergent movement forces the church to see itself as an organic system rather than a machine. Within an ecosystem, change, evolution, and adaptation are normative and expected. This is a departure from how church has been imagined and practiced in the last century.

In the last century, the Western church, and Christianity in general, were marked largely by stasis and its corollary, decline or death. While some consider "emergence" as primarily a postmodern adaptation, it can be understood to be a resurrection reality amid a decaying past, a dynamic phenomenon first explicated by the gospel writers in a pre-scientific world. Many emergent types are inclined to believe that this recent postmodern movement is largely a revaluation of pre-modern wisdom that was lost in varying degrees along history's march toward modernization.

Going back to the colloquialism above, "where the modern church put a period, the emergent movement has erased it and put a comma." The story of the church was not finished during the modern era. Emergents argue that they all have pencil and paper and are eager to continue writing. This book is an exercise in continuing to write the story of the church, specifically for Baptists. Doing so involves the integration of the past with dreams about the future that begin wearing flesh in the present. In each story below, you will encounter a Baptist who is attempting just that.

EMERGENT BAPTISTS

Emergent Baptists are those who believe there is more to God, Jesus, and God's kingdom than modern Christianity and its denominational categories have been able to define. Emergent Baptists believe the story is still unfinished, and it is incumbent upon us to participate in, and write, the narrative for our time and place. We also recognize that much of the former narrative, written by those in the last century, does not interface well with this new century and present cultural milieu. Like generations before us, we hope to take what our forefathers and mothers gave us and fashion something from it that is our own. This book contains some of our first efforts at doing so.

I am confident that some of the stories here will cause readers a level of discomfort. As you read, you may find yourself saying, "That's not Baptist!" This is a natural response since many of us have been formed in the divisive context of Baptist life where each faction believes it has defined what it means to be Baptist absolutely and with finality. This is certainly not a departure from what it means to be Baptist. After all, our tradition was forged in the fires of Separatism. Baptist identity was birthed through reform and critique of the status quo.

It is also important to keep in mind that the people who wrote the articles in this book do not believe there is a period at the end of the Baptist story. Nor do we believe that Baptist identity is ever finished. If Baptist identity is organic, it is always unfolding in process, and it will always have ample variance. In other words, an organic Baptist identity will always consist of plurality and diversity, two values that make sense to emergents.

We encourage you to read these stories of Baptist emergence with an open heart and an open mind. Contrary to what some Baptist leaders say about emergents, we are not mindless relativists with a careless, subversive agenda. We are your Baptist children and grandchildren, your Baptist brothers and sisters. We write out of a passion and a longing to cultivate something of our own from what we have been faithfully given. We may do so with a measure of prophetic edge, but we are confident that we stand in a long tradition of God's faithful in doing so.

We are also confident that many of you who read this will breathe a long, deep sigh of relief, something like, "*Finally!* There are people out there who think and feel the way I do about the life of faith." You may read the thoughts of your own heart and mind within the pages of this book. To you, we want to issue a hearty "Welcome home." It is our intent with this book that you not only engage new voices in common with yours, but that you feel you have been given both permission and space to live from your location as a Baptist "abnormally born." Call them emergent Baptists, third-way Baptists (not conservative and not liberal/moderate), or recovering Baptists, those who wrote these stories mean to encourage and give hope: encouragement for those struggling with the excitement and responsibility for writing a new narrative, and hope for those who have honored their commitment to the previous narrative but are befuddled by what is happening in the present.

Our stories are about new life that extends from the natural ending of things that cannot go on. Grief and hope should find a normal symbiosis as you interact with these writers. If we are the people of the resurrection that we claim to be, then we should have no fear of death—be it conceptual, ideological, or physical. Our collective work within these pages is a rolling of the stone away from the door, and we encourage Baptists to walk out into a new life in God's future. Perhaps the tradition forged around the practice of baptism finds itself poised at the edge of the Jordan. Our stories are dispatches from the other bank of the river.

Chapter 1

THE TIME IS NOW, THE PLACE IS NEAR

George (Tripp) Fuller III

SPACE TO EMERGE

I began to emerge during Lent of my fifth grade year, but this beginning is important because my emergence as a Baptist has been full of theology and always on the left side. I had been a Christian for a while and was a nightly Bible reader, so this particular Lent I decided that in preparation for Easter, I would read the Passion Narratives from all four Gospels. Each week I focused on a different Gospel, reading a section each night and journaling about it afterward or spending time in meditation over it (my parents taught me lectio divina at an early age). I may have been taught my love for Scripture and in particular the Gospels, but it is foundational to my identity. I cannot remember a time when I could go to sleep without reading Scripture, at first with my parents and then by myself, so as Easter neared and it became more difficult to sleep afterward, I knew something was awry. During Holy Week, I began to read through the Gospel of John, and I remember the panic of the first night of reading. Instead of stopping at the planned point, I went on right through the end, but my disturbance was not lifted. The next night I borrowed a Bible from my father's office and read through the end of all four Gospels again, but my panic continued to grow. The following night I charted out all four Gospels, and my fear reached a fevered pitch, so I called for my dad to come in my room. "Dad, my Bible is broken! The Gospels do not say the same thing, have the same people in the same places, or even have the same number of angels or people at the resurrection."

As it turns out, my Bible was not broken, but my uncritical faith that preserved a certain naiveté was gone for good. Surprisingly, at least for some of my conservative friends, my newfound critical eye became the first step on a journey that has occupied me ever since. My love for the Scriptures has not changed; in fact, I still have trouble going to sleep without reading them. Not only that, but my desire to follow Jesus in my own life, to share the good news of God's reconciling love with others, to participate in a local body of worshiping believers, and to sing a bit louder on Easter morning has not changed. The space Dad made for my question then and through school led me on a theological journey that is inseparable from my story of emergence. In fact, what emerged through the questions was a strong conviction about the gospel.

ASKING GOOD QUESTIONS

Some want to keep a gospel so disembodied
that is doesn't get involved at all
in the world it must save.
Christ is now in history.
Christ is in the womb of the people.
Christ is now bringing about
the new heavens and the new earth. —Oscar Romero[1]

There were 70,000 people in attendance, spread out over a large, gentle hill. All eyes focused forward to the bottom of the hill where the stage hosted a popular contemporary Christian band that decided in the middle of a set to enter a time of worship. Without a fuss or stager, the crowd knew what to do, and what was a rock and roll show without cursing and drugs became a time of intense worship. During the concert, the sky had grown dark, and twenty minutes into the worship set the audience was encouraged to get on their knees in prayer before God, to pray for the country and the world. This was the point when I finally arrived from my camp to the concert area. I walked up the hill, and as I looked out I saw 70,000 people on their knees in prayer. The sight moved me; the memory of all those people focused on one thing still moves me. I have long thought about that moment and asked why the world did not change after that dramatic experience. Surely a group that large with a unified vision could truly accomplish something beautiful and amazing. What were we waiting for? That was eleven years ago and counting.

The church is not running short on experiences. You can have one every day of the week in a variety of forms and places in any American city. If you have a radio or the Internet, endless resources can fill your experience quota while you drive or work when no one is watching. In spite of the effective marketing of experiences in the church, there remains a disconnect between the engaged citizen of heaven and the citizen of the earth. It may be time to ask what we are getting out of the time and energy we invest in creating our own experiences. Or better yet, what is God doing with them? The church has become a successful industry, but what are we selling? If we sell a million copies for less than they cost, we make no profit. We can do a good job at missing the point, so let us find the point. An honest assessment of the world should lead one to question the efficacy of the gospel or at least the church. If the shepherds' angelic choir was right and the good news is really "good news of great joy for all the people," then something is amiss. If the problem is not God's, then we must look to ourselves. We need to ask with all seriousness, who are we? Where are we going? What should we be doing? To address the important questions, we turn to the source of our faith and its coming.

THE GOOD NEWS OF ABBA-INTIMACY

The beginning of the good news of Jesus Christ, Son of God . . . . In those days Jesus came from Nazareth of Galilee and was baptized by John in the Jordan. And just as he was coming up out of the water, he saw the heavens torn apart and the Spirit descending like a dove on him. And a voice came from heaven, "You are my Son, the Beloved; with you I am well pleased." And the Spirit immediately drove him out into the wilderness. He was in the wilderness for forty days, tempted by Satan; and he was with the wild beasts; and the angels waited on him. (Mark 1:1, 9-13)

This passage introduces Mark's Gospel and offers an important place to begin to search for a reservoir of ecclesial identity in our age of identity crisis and identity fabrication. In these few verses, we see how Mark identifies Jesus and the foundation for Jesus' self-understanding. As the church of Jesus Christ, it is only logical that our identity search be informed by the identity given to Jesus by his first storyteller. Setting this opening to the book in its first-century context and in particular in its imperial context helps us identify Mark's expansive outlook for the God movement present in Jesus.

Mark does not begin his Gospel as a traditional Hellenistic biography by noting the character with which the author is concerned, but instead claims that this story is the beginning of the good news of Jesus Christ.[2] This simple phrase is a loaded one, for it first claims that the text is simply the start and does not contain the complete good news. Better yet, the good news is more than a text to read and digest and more than a story to hear and remember;

the good news of Jesus Christ is about more than one person's life or a past happening, but something that has begun and is still present.[3] The good news is not just an event or a singular happening; it is a life-determining reality that moves from this storied beginning to an end yet unknown.

"Good news" is not a benign term in Mark's historical context. The good news was proclaimed after a military victory and expanded to mean "the good news of peace and prosperity" following such a victory.[4] We also know that good news (also translated "good tidings" or "gospel") was used in the emperor cult and was associated with the "empire's benefits such as an emperor's birth, military conquest, or ascension to power."[5] One famous example is the Priene inscription, which originated within a decade of Jesus' birth. It declares the emperor Augustus to be the "savior" and "concludes with the line 'the birthday of the god Augustus was the *beginning* for the world of *good tidings* that came by reason of him.'"[6] Seeing that Rome pronounced "divine sanction for its empire, claiming that the gods had chosen Rome to manifest the gods' sovereignty, presence, agency, and blessings on earth," Mark's counter claim about the beginning of the gospel or good news of Jesus Christ is made quite radical.[7] In this context, the following claims that Jesus is the "Christ," the anointed king of Israel, and "Son of God" take on an even greater meaning.[8] Rome had already anointed a king for Israel and already had a "son of God" in resident. Caesar, the Herods, and the structures they represent had a gospel, and Mark set the one beginning in Jesus over against it. Regardless of the other interpretive categories at work, Mark's title for his narrative deliberately parodies the political propaganda of the reigning empire.[9]

If this is how Mark starts his Gospel, it is no wonder that it ends with Salome, Mary Magdalene, and Mary the mother of James fleeing the empty tomb after being seized by terror and amazement: "and they said nothing to anyone, for they were afraid."[10] When read in a first-century context, this fear makes perfect sense because there was already a "good news" in circulation, an anointed one on the throne, and a son of God ruling the established order. If the empty tomb of the crucified but resurrected Jesus means the good news of Jesus Christ, kingdom-proclaimer, Son of God did not die on a cross, then this story is not over and is just beginning. If the expansive claim of Mark is true, one should be fearful because the good news of Jesus is not so good for those on the beneficial take from the current arrangement under the Roman domination system. One who benefits from the imperial power structure is much more inclined to protect the world as it is. The peace of Rome is kept on the backs of the poor and the blood of resisters. Cross-building coercion is scary even if the tomb of the cross-bearer is empty. For this reason, it is important to see the second reservoir of identity in this first section. This is the reservoir that empowered the person of Jesus and gave shape to his own self-understanding.

Mark's narrative about Jesus begins with Jesus having gone to find John the baptizer at the Jordan. We do not know what caused Jesus to seek John, but something about the renewal movement of John attracted Jesus as it did many others in the Judean countryside. Baptism in the Jordan was a symbol of renewal. It echoes the exodus story in which God brought Israel out from the Egyptian domination system—a liberation symbol. John's own homiletical reference to Isaiah 40, "Prepare the way of the Lord," is an echo of the return of Israel to Jerusalem after the Babylonian exile—a reunion symbol.[11] These symbols are then tied to the practice of baptism, which, contrary to its traditional function in first-century Judaism, is here used for the remission of sin and not simply the cleansing of ritual purity.[12] In the ministry of John, you have the interplay of three metaphors of God's redemptive activity: liberation, reunion, and forgiveness of sin. Here these are mutually supporting and interpreting metaphors of a single divine reality that Jesus will identify as the kingdom of God or the God movement. No one metaphor can grasp what John offered those who came to him at the Jordan, but in his encounter with John, Jesus had a revelatory moment with the God he sought.[13]

The renewing and redemptive God presented by John is one for whom we are to wait. Mark notes that "people from the whole Judean countryside and all the people of Jerusalem were going out to him, confessing their sin," and it can be assumed that they went back to their homes, families, and lives anticipating the in-breaking of God's renewal.[14] The nature of God's imminent renewal in the preaching of John was that of judgment, and in preparation for it one repented and was baptized.[15] How Jesus ended up being baptized is not discussed in Mark, but his baptism's meaning is given before and after the event. Before the baptism, John speaks of one who is to come, an apocalyptic figure from God who will bring the Holy Spirit in a more powerful way. Presumably this was Jesus. After John baptized Jesus into the renewal movement, his experience was surely not that of forgiveness of sins, but the anointing of the Spirit. After the baptism when Jesus came out of the water, he saw the heavens tear apart, a violent theophonic image like much of the apocalyptic eschatology associated with John's preaching, but then the Spirit descends on him like a dove.[16] In this experience, which only Jesus and the reader witness, a voice comes from heaven and says, "You are my Son, the Beloved, with you I am well pleased."[17] In this moment Jesus realizes his identity before God and is forever shaped by it. At this moment as never before, Jesus receives the anointing and filling of the Spirit, like others in the "Spirit-filled stream of Judaism" before him.[18] From this moment to the cross, Jesus no longer expects God to come with apocalyptic divine fury like John, but instead knows God in a more intimate and relational way; he knows God as *Abba*. The dramatic contrasts in the ministries of Jesus and John are based here, in this moment where God breaks open the heavens to draw near to Jesus.[19] The imminent one whose kingdom he will announce is first the loving Abba, not a wrathful judge, who knows the names of all God's children. The level of intimacy between God and Jesus, who now is self-consciously given the identity of Son and Beloved of God, causes a dramatic shift in the conceptual vision of God between John and Jesus. Jesus did not keep this a secret; instead, God as Abba forever shaped the ministry and life of Jesus. To be a disciple of Jesus was to be committed in life and in prayer to God, sharing in the abba-intimacy of the Son.

The church of Jesus needs to take these two markers of identity seriously. If the gospel of Jesus Christ, Son of God, was a challenge to the character, method, message, and reign of the ruling powers of the first century, then those who wish to follow Jesus today should not be surprised or shocked to find that the gospel remains a story of revolution. The domestication of the Christian faith is clearly an activity in which the church invests a good deal of time, but to what end? At what point will we have made the gospel so palatable to the power wielders that it is no longer the gospel of Jesus Christ, but mammon? Though a gross understatement, the gospel of Jesus Christ is not empire compatible and domination friendly. The reason this is true is much more than a historical argument about the intention of Mark; it is an argument about the character of God. If God is as loving as Jesus said he was, desiring intimate relationships of healing empowerment with all, and if God was definitively revealed in the person and work of Jesus, then God does not rule like Caesar nor even as a slightly more benevolent Caesar, but as a loving parent.[20] For God to seek out and initiate abba-intimacy with humanity is to reshape the notion of power in contrast to the one holding sway over the world. This world-holding sway occurs and thrives in dehumanized coercive relationships. To follow Jesus is to seek out and announce to the dehumanized their favor and friendship with God.

The church can begin to take the contrasting notions of power seriously by first taking the full humanity of all into account. If our life together is transformed as Jesus' was after his baptism by the abba-intimacy of God, then our understanding of power and people would be shaped by the vision of God that Jesus revealed. Relationships of dehumanization exist when one destroys the otherness of the Other, the dehumanized one refuses to give the Other the space and possibility of differentiation without violence, and the Other is judged, given value, and named by the dehumanizer. This was the pattern of Rome; it organized and justified relentless exploitation of humans by treating them as anything but. Think of the rhetoric of the Hutu radio during the ethnic genocide in Rwanda, "we must kill the Tutsi *cockroaches*." Dehumanization can transcend the socio-political sphere into any relational network, with domestic violence being an example of its darkest form. When dehumanization occurs, one has claimed the position of final arbiter of reality and interpreter of identity, turning what should be a mutually informing and enriching relationship between peoples into a hemorrhaging cycle of violence. In the relational nexus of a dehumanizing reality, both parties are impoverished. The violated individuals are withheld their own personhood, which is abused, and violators seek to establish themselves on their own accord. Violators, like those they violate, are dehumanized because a person's humanity is only found in going out of the self in relationship with others. Violators have turned recklessly inward. They have sought to say what "no one can ever say . . . , for no one is God." They have said, "I am who I am."[21]

The first step to finding our identity as the church in the pattern of Jesus is opening ourselves to others, including God. If this story is true, then opening ourselves to a relationship with God will not reveal a dehumanizing God. Many live in fear that God does not value the otherness of God's own creation and that God demands conformity and possession over the gift of respect and affection. Many fear because they have a false concept of God in which God has not chosen relationship with creation but uses God's infinite otherness to annihilate the possibility of freedom necessary for a true relationship of love. This first step of the church is to reject this concept of God as an idol. When the heavens are torn apart and God comes near, we do not hear the march of God's apocalyptic army, but the voice of one who first invites us into an identity as the beloved of God. Through our friendship "in Christ," we come to know God first as *Abba*. The first step is to find our identity "in Christ" and make our foundational claim: we are the beloved of God.

The second step is based on the observation that with a humanizing God and a church of God-belovedness, our relational nexus of identity giving and receiving has to be expanded. Because God is the creator of all, by being in relationship to God, our relational network has become infinitely open to the entire diversity of God's creation. The life of the church must struggle to preserve this openness and the freedom of a relationship established by and in Abba. It is precisely this concept of God, established in the Abba-intimacy and belovedness of creation, that gives rise to the expansion of the ministry of Jesus to the marginalized and eventually turns a Jewish sect into a global community. The radial openness and freedom God gives God's beloved is foundational for the movement of God in the world. God is love, and "true love nurtures wholeness, granting to the beloved the authenticity and independence of his existence. Creative love does not ask the beloved for his dependency but for his personhood," and so "the eyes of love perceive yet unrealized possibilities."[22] When God is first known as Abba, the relational stance of God must be re-imaged, especially when omnipotent coercive compliance with the divine will is the inherited image. The love of Abba changes the way identity is formed because "love, on the one hand, envisions in the beloved the destiny of his life and the promise of life's fulfillment. Love views the beloved with the eyes of God. Yet love too respects the beloved. He anticipates that the potential will be realized through the other person's own decision and effort. Love can support, but it does not seek to control, the struggle towards realization."[23] When Jesus came to a realization of his own identity in God, he was tempted but did not waver because even in the desert of confrontation, Abba was near. With an openness to God established and an identity as the beloved claimed and expanded to all in the relational nexus of Abba, having been tempted to forsake this vision that challenges all dehumanizing powers, Jesus speaks his first words. These words come out of the experience of baptism, temptation, and an identity found in abba-intimacy.

THE EMBRACING ABBA AND THE GOD MOVEMENT

Now after John was arrested, Jesus came to Galilee, proclaiming the good news of God, and saying, "The time is fulfilled, and the kingdom of God has come near; repent, and believe in the good news." (Mark 1:14-15)

Every Gospel has a powerful sermon at the beginning. Luke has Jesus reading the scroll of Isaiah that says, "the Spirit of the Lord is upon me, because he has anointed me to bring good news to the poor. He has sent me to proclaim release to the captives and recovery of sight to the blind, to let the oppressed go free, to proclaim the year of the Lord's favor."[24] After reading this, he proclaimed the Scripture fulfilled in their hearing. In Matthew, the first discourse of Jesus is the legendary Sermon on the Mount, a kind of manifesto for the followers of Jesus. Here in Mark, Jesus gives a one-line zinger of a sermon that contains the mystery of the mission of Jesus. There is no challenge to the notion that the kingdom of God was the central symbol that determined Jesus' preaching and interpreted Jesus' deeds.[25] It is important to remember that the kingdom of God finds its "concrete content" as it "emerges from his ministry and activity as a whole," which requires one to interpret no pericope alone.[26] To grasp its meaning or at least its mystery contextually, the brief yet telling narrative structure matters.[27]

John has been arrested in this Scripture, and so Jesus starts to preach. John was not arrested by just anyone; he was arrested by Herod, a Roman-appointed anointed one of Israel, for challenging Herod's way of ruling in his preaching. The connection is easily made when one recalls the power-packed beginning of the gospel. The good news of Jesus Christ is going to continue the challenge of the domination system's power established in John. The resistance will end, as did John's life, in a hostile confrontation, arrest, and death. The contrast between the two comes in the middle of verse 14: Jesus took the prophetic mantle of John to the people. Empowered by the spirit of Abba and the universal horizon of love for a God who is loving parent, Jesus ceases to preach a gospel at a riverbank on the margins of society, but instead takes God's message to the margins. This distinction is supremely important for understanding the meaning of Jesus' sermon. It must be heard differently when the God it comes from is known as Abba and not apocalyptic judge. Even though God still has the same roles, here king and judge, Abba as king and Abba as judge mean something completely different. This difference is acted upon when Jesus takes the message of the kin-dom of God to the beloved of God—the captive, blind, poor, and oppressed.[28] Knowing God as Abba makes the nature of the loving parent foundational for understanding the nature of God. A God who desires abba-intimacy does not stay on the margins with a message of coming judgment, but goes into and seeks the margins of the world and announces good news of jubilee.

For followers of Christ, this distinction is not only theological but also practical. If we are to follow Jesus, we cannot be a people of the margins and live as aliens to our Abba's world. When John left the scene and Jesus stood up, Jesus did not take up residence in John's post on the outskirt of society but shifted the focus of the mission from margin living to margin embracing. Jesus did not continue to operate with the rigid sacred secular divide he inherited, but engaged all of creation as the beloved of Abba. When the coming reign is Abba's, it is not a reign of fear and terror but of hope and reconciliation. These central categories, hope and reconciliation, must shape our life together. When a community is no longer founded on fear of God's coming terror, it is less likely to define itself in the negative and separate from the world. Instead, a community that hopes in God's reconciliation defines itself in the positive, by announcing in word and way the center of the community. Inherently, hope in reconciliation gives birth to a people of hospitality because every movement of openness is a movement toward the horizon of hope, namely the realization of Abba's reconciling reign. The church as an institution has often failed to be on the margins where the kin-dom is found. It is easy for each new generation of leaders to decide that what the last generation said and where the last generation lived is the only appropriate way. Against this prevailing reality Jesus invites us to follow him into the margins and refuse to be marginal. Refusing marginal living does not presume we would not be marginalized; after all, the movement of God led Jesus to Jerusalem, where his marginalization took the shape of a cross. Embracing the margins of society means keeping the focus outside ourselves. Like the church, Jesus was tempted to stay where God first became inti-mately vivid, take up the ministry of John by simply stepping into his shoes, and tame down the message to appease John's executioners, but Jesus did none of these. Empowered by the Spirit, we too are called to share in the mission of God for the world, which leaves no one where he or she started. The mission of God is the coming of God's kingdom in the world, and this is the substance of Jesus' own mission—one the church shares.[29] Simply put, the concern here is that the church not confuse itself with the kingdom of God. The two are not synonyms.[30] Instead, the church is to find its identity as it anticipates and participates in this sacred reality.

If we are to hear Jesus correctly in verse 15, we will not imagine that prior to any of the ministry activities recorded in the Gospels, Jesus went around Galilee just preaching a single sentence on a solo mission. Instead, this one line should be understood as Mark's "summarizing in advance the

whole Galilean ministry," which not only included teaching about the kingdom but also the healings, the exorcisms, and the community that was
present throughout.[31] It is also important to remember when thinking about
the content of the kingdom of God that in the Gospels, Jesus sends out the
disciples to announce and participate in its coming.[32] The kingdom is a
movement of God, the definitive God movement.[33] Often discussions of the
kingdom miss the most important part of all: this is the reality followers of
Jesus are not only to anticipate but in which they are also to participate. The
kingdom of God or the God movement is to be the determining reality for
the mission of Jesus and his followers. Because this reality is participatory
and not something the church possesses, the effectiveness of our life together
is related to our vision. The content of our kin-dom vision is the content of
our kin-dom living. To be Jesus' church, we need to get Jesus' vision in our
hearts, in our minds, and in our lives. Not only is the God movement the
centerpiece of Jesus' ministry, but it is also the content of the good news
itself. Thus, Jesus' proclamation of the present activity of the God movement
is the good news.

There is no confusion among scholars that the God movement was the
focal point of the teaching of Jesus. While the exact meaning of the phrase
itself remains a debate, there are a few widely held agreements, namely that
God's kingdom was for earth, involved its transformation, and was both a
religious and political statement.[34] John Meier, a centrist scholar, describes
the consensus this way: "the symbol of God's kingly rule increasingly came to
be connected (in the first century) with the hope that God would bring an
end to the present state of the world and would embark upon his full definitive rule over his rebellious creation and people."[35] The first verse of Mark
shares in the politico-religious connotation of the gospel that we cannot miss
here, but in addition to what has already been noted it would be good to recognize that "Rome referred to itself not as an 'empire,' but as a 'kingdom.'"[36]
There was already a kingdom present in Galilee when Jesus announced the
presence of God's; locally it was the kingdom of Herod who ruled under the
auspices of Rome's kingdom. "Kingdom" was a thoroughly political word,
unlike other options available to Jesus such as "people," "community," "society," or "family of God." In fact, what made Jesus distinct was not his talk
about kingdom and politics or God and religion, but the "of" he put
between the two.[37] Caesar had already combined the two realities. Herod
supported the world ruled by the deified Caesar; Jesus proclaimed an alternative reality to their reigning. It is no surprise that the foundational message of

one who died on a revolutionary's cross began with the proclamation of a rival kingdom. The domination system knew that "for Jesus, 'the Kingdom of God' raised a politico-religious or religio-political question: to whom did the world belong, and how, depending on the answer, should it be run?"[38] Recognizing that Jesus did not exist in a world that neatly divided religion and politics, we can begin to understand just how radically presumptuous it was for a peasant of the oppressed class to have an experience of God that led him to pronounce that the time is now and the place of God's righting of the world is near.

For the church in the democratic first world, the mixing of religion and politics is uncomfortable. Not only are these subjects rarely discussed unless the company is safe, but when Christians take political stands for religious reasons, they often go from Bible to political party. There is rarely any discourse within the church about our socio-political life that does not automatically go to a political agenda and party. The theological content is not developed for social transformation of the church and the relational networks in which its members exist, but focuses instead on rallying people for votes. The use of religion for political power has impoverished the radical message of the God movement, implying that the kingdom can come on one Tuesday in November every two years. The God movement as Jesus taught and lived is an all-encompassing reality that shapes and reshapes the body politic of every person who chooses to live in its transformative presence. To focus on a single issue or to limit one's involvement with an issue to the voting booth is to miss the point entirely. Jesus had no political power, yet to those marginalized people who cried out to God for relief, he said, "The time is fulfilled." If it was not a constitution, bill of rights, or voting box that empowered Jesus to make this revolutionary statement, where did it come from? The answer is the history of Israel and Jesus' own understanding of it that developed out of his experience of God as Abba.[39]

For Jesus, the God movement was the good news, and while it was a highly positive reality, we cannot deny that it was highly critical. To say that there was a new kingdom present and that it was God's was to judge the present reign of domination. To say entrance to the God movement entailed repentance and the giving of oneself to this alternative reality meant the current order was not sufficient. The kingdom of God is what the world would be like if Abba were in charge and the domination system were not. While the God movement was confrontational to the reigning powers, it came unlike any other kingdom. Rome's kingdom came from the deployment of legions and the building of crosses; God's came from the divine initiative of grace and the bearing of crosses. The ways and means of Rome's empire building are absent in the Abba movement, but it is precisely their absence that enables God's kingdom to be the divine answer for history's questions. God's coming is not a path filled with victims of a sacred sword or piles of the nameless collateral damage.

The issue that must be dealt with by the church today, which has its own history of baptizing empire building into the practice of God's kingdom, is power. Too often the church has described the God whose kingdom Jesus brought to be a more powerful and benevolent version of Caesar's. While at the surface we think this is an appropriate compliment to God, in the end it is a metaphysical compliment that is both detrimental to God's character and subversive to our own responsibility. It is detrimental to God's character for us to speak as if God's power has the nature of an imperial military force that imposes its will regardless of the desire and well-being of the occupants. Are we to confess that the God who is love loves by force? Do we want the ideal of Love, presumably God's, to be one that does not recognize the identity, value, or even the otherness of the other? If this conception of Love's power is allowed to stand, God looks more like a lustful criminal than faithful partner and the church looks more like the violated victim than the empowered bride. This concept has absolutely nothing to do with the cross. The cross stands as a reminder to the church that its power is other than that of history's cross-builders, for we are the people of the cross-bearer.

Jesus began his mission with a message that there was no more waiting; the God movement was already present and in the process of becoming. What Jesus was proclaiming "was not just a vision or a theory but a praxis and a communal program" that was open to all who would respond.[40] By understanding the theological density of the first half of Jesus' sermon, "The time is fulfilled, and the kingdom of God has come near," we can better understand the nature of response that was called for. Jesus went to the marginal people of a colonialized and exploited area and told them God's answer to their fractured reality was present. In doing so, Jesus put hope in the present and the resurrection made it a permanent fixture on the horizon of history. What should not be missed is the nature and order of the response. First comes repentance and then belief. Each of these concepts requires an explanation from the context of the narrative.

The Abba experience initiates Jesus' movement to the people; there he announces that the God movement is already a present reality and that it is good news that is really good. God is love supreme and intends belonging and belovedness for all. The Abba movement is first and foremost a gift. The kingdom is a gift that comes from God and through the grace of God. The origin of the God movement "is the absolute loving initiative of God, which is neither forced nor can be forced—this being both unnecessary and impossible—by human actions."[41] Humanity cannot give birth to an answer to history's questions. Said another way, apart from the good news of Jesus being the actual redemptive movement of God in the world, it would simply be another failed human attempt that would end up changing who was on the good end of the power exchange. Because the kingdom Jesus brought was Abba's, it was good news for all creation and came out of the essence of God's own being. Humanity could neither create nor initiate a relational system for creation that could bring justice for all, so it must be received as a gift. The gifted nature of the kin-dom does not eliminate human action or ethical responsibility, but it does create a wholly new framework for them.

When Jesus proclaimed the God movement, he extended God's invitation of participation to humanity. The response to the gift is first repentance. The church has often managed to commodify the God movement and in doing so has wanted belief to come before repentance. When this is done, not only is kingdom repentance impoverished, but so is belief. Belief, when made the initial response, becomes a cognitive act and not something that changes the whole being of a person, not something that includes the shifting of allegiance from one kingdom to another. Many in the church in the first world have made belief the ability to pass God's true-false test for eternal security and effectively made the good news about heaven and one's personal destination. It is as if Jesus taught us to pray, "Thy kingdom come, thy will be done, so we can forsake earth and enter heaven." This is not the gospel of the kingdom or the good news of the God movement. Jesus had complete confidence that God had heaven under control and that God's activity was on earth. Therefore he taught us to pray that God's kingdom come and will be done *on earth*. The coming of the kingdom and the fulfillment of God's will are synonyms. If this is true, believing Jesus' gospel is not simply a cognitive act. That is why Jesus' first word is repentance—a transformation of one's whole being—and then belief—the lived practice of trust in this new reality. Jesus is not asking people to walk the aisle, check a box on a response card, respond to spiritual laws, or walk down the Roman Road; he is saying, "change your whole way of thinking, acting, loving, and living because a new order is here and coming, it is the *Abba* movement, God's gift to creation."[42]

In commodifying the gospel, the church has created its own, one that extinguishes God's gift and abrogates the participation in the relational gospel reality. The church does not need any new marketing strategies; it needs a return to its mission, the sharing and living of the good news. The gospel of Jesus' church should be the gospel of Jesus. "The time is now, and the kingdom of God has come near; repent, and believe in the good news."

A return to gospel living, or participation in the anticipatory fulfillment of creation, will threaten the gospel that has resulted in the colonial history of the Western church. Some contemporary visions of the kingdom fall short by putting its fulfillment completely in the future; this misunderstands the gift of God and impoverishes the task of the church. The scope of a completely future kingdom is narrow and leaves people to complacent waiting and possibly feverish sharing of a personal salvation that trivializes the landscape of suffering in history. They may use the language of good news, gospel, salvation, and kingdom, but it is not the one of which Jesus spoke. There is another failed kingdom vision in the church, one that makes the kingdom of God a completely present reality. It has two major forms, the existentialist kingdom that personalizes the kingdom message to be simply about becoming individually awakened to the divine reality, and the industrial kingdom that believes the kingdom to be the product of human social transformation and fails to distinguish between the coming of the kingdom and a political platform. This perversion of the kingdom message does not recognize that it is God's kingdom. The kingdom begins with God and not a human remedy to political ills, and because it is God's kingdom it exists for the entire relational nexus of God. The point that must be made in examining these mistaken visions is not that the kingdom does not include social transformation, personal transformation, or hope for the future, but simply that it is *all* these things. Because the God movement is the gift of God, humans cannot give it. The church is not a gift-giving body, but a gift-bearing body. It is to be the community in which the gift of God is celebrated, anticipated, and practiced but never given. The kin-dom of God is a movement, a relational nexus that includes all God's creation and moves toward its completion. In Jesus Christ, who was the prophet of the God movement and was raised from the dead after the domination system rejected Abba's vision for the world, is found the promise that neither individuals in their brokenness, social systems in their twistedness, nor history in its violence have the last word. God's Word, Jesus Christ, the presence of the divine embrace into the God movement, is the "cosmic incarnation of God."[43] Creation is neither left forsaken by God nor the locale of a divine invasion, but the place of Abba's coming. History is neither left to its own promise nor wiped clean at a moment of intervention, but is the space God created for the loving inclusion of the world into God's own being. The beginning of the good news of Jesus Christ, Son of God, was that God is Abba and God's movement of hope is now and the place is near. Repent. Believe.

Exactly how do we re-image the gospel to make God's identity as Abba define the character of God and to make the God movement found in Jesus and his ministry shape the nature of the church's mission? This is a precarious endeavor in a postcolonial world. As followers of Jesus, how can we practice and share the gospel as individuals and communities in a world whose landscape is littered with signs of Christian-led and supported colonialism? What offer can we make, and what vision can we share? The means by which the relational gospel took shape in the ministry of Jesus should advise the church today that desires passionate commitment to God. It is my hope that, as the church emerges from its theological and missiological stupor, it will find its identity by joining the God movement and letting that emerging terrain name the church.

Notes

1. Oscar Romero, *The Violence of Love* (Mary Knoll NY: Orbis Books, 1988) 102.

2. Eugene Boring, *Mark: A Commentary* (Louisville: Westminster John Knox Press, 2006) 30.

3. Hans Urs Von Balthasar makes a similar connection when he states, "The mission of Jesus has no conceivable temporal beginning. But as it unfolds through historical time, it enters increasingly into history. It awaits God's signal for its fulfillment not only purely from within; it also awaits it from without, because the mission will be fulfilled essentially in history no less than in interior inspiration" (*Theo-Drama: Theological Dramatic Theory*, vol. 3 of *Dramatic Personae: Persons in Christ*, trans. Graham Harrison [San Francisco: Ignatius Press, 1992] 178).

4. Ibid., 30.

5. Warren Carter, *The Roman Empire and the New Testament: An Essential Guide* (Nashville: Abingdon Press, 2006) 90.

6. Boring, *Mark*, 30, emphasis mine.

7. Carter, *The Roman Empire and the New Testament*, 90.

8. Some manuscripts do not have "Son of God," but, if kept, it is an addition of a title claimed by the Roman emperor and not simply a metaphysical statement about the person of Jesus.

9. Gilberto Da Silva Gorgulho, "Biblical Hermenutics," in *Mysterium Liberationis: Fundametal Concepts of Liberation Theology*, ed. Ignacio Ellacuria and Sobrino (Maryknoll NY: Orbis Books, 1993) 130.

10. Mark 16:8.

11. Mark 1:3.

12. While it is unclear if Jesus continued the practice of baptism in his own ministry, he did share John's critique if not rejection of the temple cult. By taking a purity cleansing ritual and giving it the function of the temple, John supplants the authority of the temple and its centrality for the life of his followers. Beyond being the source of a theological disagreement, the temple was a vestige of power that Rome via the High Priest and company used to keep the Jewish people passive to their own exploitation.

13. There is nothing in Mark that should lead one to think Jesus had a self-understanding of his messianic vocation prior to his baptism. Saying this does not however require an adoptionistic Christology or eliminate a christological affirmation of incarnation. It is only a christological affirmation about Jesus that validates the methodological assumptions throughout this essay.

14. Mark 1:5. The expansiveness of positive response probably does not extend this far, though we do know from the writings of Josephus that John was a public figure.

15. Matthew and Luke, presumably following Q, emphasize the level to which apocalyptic judgment characterizes the preaching of John.

16. Boring, *Mark*, 44.

17. Mark 1:11.

18. Marcus Borg, *Jesus: Uncovering the Life, Teachings, and Relevance of a Religious Revolutionary* (New York: Harper San Francisco, 2006) 122.

19. Jürgen Moltmann, *The Way of Jesus Christ: Christology in Messianic Dimensions*, trans. Margaret Kohl (Minneapolis: Fortress Press, 1993) 88–91. Here Moltmann is attentive to the theological importance of the commonly addressed contrasts. He locates these contrasts, as I do, in the identity of Jesus who knows God as Abba.

20. Alfred North Whitehead made a similar observation when he said, "When the Western world accepted Christianity, Caesar conquered; and the received text of Western theology was edited by his lawyers. . . . The brief Galilean vision of humility flickered throughout the ages, uncertainly. In the official formulation of the religion it has assumed the trivial form of the mere attribution to the Jews that they cherished a misconception about their Messiah. But the deeper idolatry, of fashioning God in the image of the Egyptian, Persian, and Roman imperial rulers was retained. The Church gave unto God the attributes which belonged exclusively to Caesar" (*Process and Reality*, corrected ed. [New York: The Free Press, 1978] 342).

21. Jürgen Moltmann, *The Spirit of Life: A Universal Affirmation* (Minneapolis: Fortress Press, 1992) 25.

22. Wolfhart Pannenberg, *Theology and the Kingdom of God* (Philadelphia: The Westminster Press, 1969) 118.

23. Ibid., 119.

24. Luke 4:18-19.

25. John P. Meier, *A Marginal Jew: Mentor, Message, and Miracles* (New York: Doubleday, 1994) 348–51.

26. Edward Schillebeeckx, *Jesus: An Experiment in Christology* (New York: Crossroad, 1979) 143.

27. For a discussion on the differing narrative contexts of this saying in the other Gospels, see Schillebeeckx, *Jesus*, 430–34.

28.Replacing the "g" in "kingdom" with a dash is a symbolic removal of the masculine assumptions tied to God and God's rule, and the imperial implications of the wpords "king" and "kingdom." God's movement transcends gender and empire. It is also a move that puts an emphasis on humanity's kinship and familial connection.

29. As Karl Barth rightly observes, "'God so loved'—not the Christian, but—'the world.' 'I am the light of the world,' says the Lord, and by His own self-giving He passes the light on to His disciples: 'Ye are the light of the world!' It is the duty of the real Church to tell and show the world what it does not yet know. This does not mean that the real Church's mission is to take the whole or even half the world to task. It would be the servant of quite a different Master if it were to set itself up as the accuser of its brethren. Its mission is not to say 'No,' but to say 'Yes'; a strong 'Yes' to the God who, because there are 'godless' men, has not thought and does not think of becoming a 'manless' God—and a strong 'Yes' to man, for whom, with no exception, Jesus Christ died and rose again. How extraordinary the Church's preaching, teaching, ministry, theology, political guardianship and missions would be, how it would convict itself of unbelief in what it says, if it did not proclaim to all men that God is not against man but for man. It need not concern itself with the 'No' that must be said to human presumption and human sloth. This 'No' will be quite audible enough when as the real Church it concerns itself with the washing of feet and nothing else. This is the obedience which it owes to its Lord in this world." (Karl Barth, "The Real Church," in *Against the Stream: Shorter Post-War Writings 1946–52* [London: SCM Press, 1954] 73)

30. Wolfhart Pannenberg advances this distinction with great precision: "Christ points the Church toward the Kingdom of God that is beyond the Church. To the degree that the Church follows his pointing and heeds his reminder, the Kingdom of God will manifest itself through the Church. But note that this is quite different from attributing to the Church in its established structures the dignity of being the Kingdom of Christ. The rule of Christ is effected wherever man becomes aware of the coming Kingdom of God and lives in accord with that awareness. This may happen in the Church. It should be expected to happen in the Church. But the rule of Christ cannot be identified with the Church's existence as a organized community in the world. The theological identification of the Church with the Kingdom of Christ has all too often served the purposes of ecclesiastical officials who are not attuned to the Kingdom of God. Many Christians, especially church leaders, like to think they are in possession of the truth, or at least that they possess the ultimate criterion of the truth. Because they feel themselves to be indispensably related to the very Kingdom of Christ, they fail to recognize the provisional character of all ecclesiastical organizations. They are unable to stand humbly before the coming Kingdom of God that is going to bring about the final future of the world. They are blinded to the ways in which even now, proleptically, the future manifests itself in the world (and not just in the Church, nor even always through the Church). Precisely because the Church mistakes herself for the present form of the Kingdom, God's rule has often had to manifest itself in the secular world outside, and frequently against, the Church." (Pannenberg, *Theology and the Kingdom of God*, 78–79)

31. Boring, *Mark*, 51.

32. See Luke 10:4-9; Matt 10:8-11; Mark 6:7-13.

33. The "God movement" is the most frequent phrase I use to describe the kingdom of God. Clarence Jordan frequently referred to it as such. This particular phrase was chosen because it emphasizes the relational nature of the kingdom, lacks the colonial/hierarchical title of kingdom, keeps the political edge with a more contemporary feel, and creates a linguistic openness to the abba experience defining the character of God over human expectations of kinghood.

34. See Wendell Willis, ed., *The Kingdom of God in 20th-Century Interpretation* (Peabody MA: Hendrickson, 1987), and Borg, *Jesus*, 186–87.

35. Meier, *A Marginal Jew*, 348.

36. Borg, *Jesus*, 186.

37. John Dominic Crossan, *God and Empire: Jesus Against Rome, Then and Now* (New York: Harper Collins, 2007) 117.

38. Ibid.

39. I like Walter Wink's observation that "Jesus brought to fruition the prophetic longing for the 'kingdom of God'—an expression we might paraphrase as 'God's domination-free order'" (*The Powers that Be: Theology for a New Millennium* [New York: Doubleday, 1998] 64).

40. Crossan, *God and Empire*, 118.

41. Jon Sobrino, *Jesus the Liberator: A Historical-Theological View* (Mary Knoll NY: Orbis, 2004) 76.

42. Clarence Jordan gives a similar paraphrase in *The Substance of Faith and other Cotton Patch Sermons*, ed. Dallas Lee (New York: Association Press, 1972) 59–60.

43. Jürgen Moltmann, *Jesus Christ for Today's World* (Minneapolis: Fortress Press, 1994) 24.

Chapter 2

A SPIRIT-RESPONSE READING OF SCRIPTURE

Ed Cyzewski

"God said it. I believe it. That settles it."

This bumper-sticker Christianity described my approach to the Bible and to theology as I entered college. The Bible was a straightforward collection of truth that one could uncover through diligent reading. Once I uncovered the truth of Scripture, I spent most of my time defending my findings. Never mind making disciples; I was a warrior—crusader on more ambitious days—for the truth of God. My adversaries included people who believed in evolution or salvation by works, and those who challenged the tenet of predestination. I spent hours debating my opponents.

No one told me point blank to be combative. No one commanded me to spend so much time arguing with fellow Christians or verbally assaulting nonbelievers. It was in the air I breathed: I saw my friends do it, I heard preachers on the radio talk about doing it, and I ended up using the Bible as a weapon to defend the truth. We spent time in youth group arguing with one another, and even with our leaders on occasion.

We figured the truth was obvious for anyone with eyes to see. It was revealed in the pages of Scripture, conveniently numbered with chapters and verses. With highlighter in hand, I could open the Bible, find the truth, and add a yellow glow.

And that was that.

If anyone doubted the truth that I believed, I resorted to attacks and debates because the other person was clearly in error. The truth of Scripture was there to be believed, so we were the defenders of biblical truth, and the disagreeing person was under the influence of something other than God's Spirit and a commitment to truth.

In my mind, it was unacceptable to have the wrong theology and risk being called a heretic. The only problem was that the heretics were those who disagreed with my theology.

I remember a Bible study in which a friend of mine—a relatively new Christian at the time—taught on law and grace. He began to talk about the importance of obeying the law. I smelled a rat.

"But wait," I said. "The law has been fulfilled in Jesus. Why do we have to try to obey it?"

He politely acknowledged my challenge and began to work through some explanations. In retrospect, I realize he was lost, fumbling over terms and concepts. Unfortunately, he became flustered and sought to buy time by talking. At one key point he said, "God does have a law and you're under it."

I pounced with the ferocity of an inquisitor. "That's not possible! We're under grace and not the law!" I had the verses at hand to back up my point.

Things didn't go well after that.

I look back with shame now at the way I attacked my friend, trying to smoke out a heretic and affirm my own reading of the Bible. Even if I was technically advocating orthodox Christian doctrine, I did not show love to my friend; instead, I made my words a clanging gong that did little to edify anyone that evening. However, back then, things were clear-cut and black and white for me. The Bible was a neat collection of theology that its students could figure out if they were honest and committed to finding the truth. My ideal was to become a walking treasury of Scripture knowledge who knew the Bible forward and backward, deftly guiding others through the finer points of Scripture. What could be better than having a vast arsenal of truth at my disposal for every single situation?

As evidenced by my confrontational approach to Bible study, I used to have an imbalanced notion of Christianity. Of course we always need to study the Bible and of course some interpretations are more valid than others, but I made the mistake of elevating a book over a person, knowing truth rather than living it, and placing the Bible ahead of Jesus, who commanded us to love one another. While the Bible will always be of central importance to the Christian faith, things can fall apart when we place a higher emphasis on the Bible and our doctrines than we do on a relationship with Jesus Christ and living out our faith. This is a fine point that needs some explanation.

The Supremacy of God

At the time of my friend's study, the Bible was the foundation of my Christian faith. It supplied all the information I needed, superseding the authority of traditions, science, and anything else that appeared to set itself up against the word of God. This meant I was deeply interested in preserving the authority of the Bible. In fact, if anyone disagreed with my interpretation of the Bible, there was no recourse but to argue with that person since I believed purity of doctrine is a necessity in a world where the Bible is at the center of the Christian faith.

Unfortunately, Jesus didn't quite agree with my assessment.

Jesus said the Scriptures testify concerning him, Paul said Christ is the foundation, and the author of Hebrews calls Jesus the author and finisher of our faith. So it seems that while the Bible is important and central to Christianity, the goal of the Bible is pointing us toward Jesus. While we desperately need the Bible, there was something inherently wrong with the way I used the Bible to attack my opponents. In light of this, I needed to rethink the way I read, interpreted, and applied the narratives, poems, oracles, and letters of Scripture. Navigating this issue consumed my years in college and seminary, though I'll be the first to admit I made my fair share of mistakes along the way.

An Evolving View of Scripture

My fledgling arsenal of truth was put to the test when I went to a Christian college and sought to defend my interpretations of the Bible. A theological arms race ensued as I amassed verses to back up my interpretations, always trying to keep ahead of my doctrinal opponents.

I was surrounded by Christians with different beliefs. Of my closest friends, one was a Church of God amillennialist, another a Methodist who believed in miracles, and the third a house church guy who talked about experiencing the "presence of God." My world was shaken as we talked things through. I wasn't always interested in understanding their views. In fact, I was quite content to spend my time trying to pick apart their views rather than hearing them out.

Why was I so bothered with different interpretations of the Bible? At the time, I didn't appreciate the complexities of interpreting the Bible. I could not imagine that another Christian, committed to the truth, could read the same chapters and verses but come up with a different interpretation, citing other passages, cultural differences, the leading of the Holy Spirit, or literary features that called my own views into question.

Throughout my first couple of years in college, I managed to defend my beliefs, protecting myself from various traditions threatening the authority of my theology. I sat through long debates in my dorm, attacking anyone who doubted the accuracy of my pure reading of Scripture. Theology was clearly presented in each biblical book, pieced together like a puzzle that forms a neat mosaic of Christian beliefs. I wasn't interested in listening to these Christians who challenged not only my beliefs, but how I arrived at them. The things I thought were even worse than what I said.

While I tried to demolish every argument—conveniently forgetting that Scripture didn't give me license to use it like a weapon against fellow Christians—cracks began to appear in my theology. The most important belief to go was the incompatibility of Christianity and evolution. In my previous reading of Genesis, there was no room for the theory of evolution. God created everything in six days, he made Adam and Eve, and they somehow managed to populate the entire earth. End of story. Thanks but no thanks, science.

Then a friend at college told me that he believed the Bible and evolution are both true. He and his father are also brilliant scientists. I don't know why I never thought of this possibility before, but he surprised me, leaving me speechless. He explained that the beginning of Genesis is most likely a poem and that interpreters are divided on exactly how to understand it. You could just as well believe that God created everything over an undetermined period of time, and that evolution took place within God's creation design. This felt like mixing ice cream and cow manure, or however that saying goes, but I let him go on.

He shared that the Bible talks about everything being created according to its kind, but doesn't specify how everything was made. In fact, he believed that micro-evolution, evolution within species, provided a perfectly plausible explanation for the passages in Genesis. In the end, though, he emphasized that this doesn't make the Bible true or false. The Bible presents two creation stories as it is, so it's hard enough to read them both literally. We may never figure out the best way to gel science and the Bible, but it was not an issue over which we should lose our faith.

This was not a hill to die on.

I was shocked. After investing so much time and energy into refuting evolution, I didn't quite know how to respond. My friend genuinely persuaded me, but agreeing with him meant stepping away from a matter I placed front and center in the Christian faith. As it turned out, the Bible could survive without my attacks on evolution. To be honest, I was also relieved because I've never liked studying science. Genesis 1–3 could be a poem of some sort, evolution could be whatever it wanted, and I could get on with the call of Jesus to be his witness. After guarding the Bible as the foundation for Christianity, I began to learn that while the Bible is true and reliable, my interpretations are not infallible, and many of the issues I considered important are not as important as living in the truth of the gospel message as it unfolds in Scripture.

Instead of fighting to protect the Bible, we are called by Jesus to be his witnesses and to live in the truth of Scripture. The Bible doesn't need to be defended as much as it needs to be lived. At the center of Christianity we have the triune God—Father, Son, and Spirit. Christianity didn't need me to defend the Bible because it is the living God who keeps our faith going, not my proofs against evolution.

It's not a tragedy that people doubt the Bible. There will always be skeptics. The real tragedy would be Christians who use the Bible as a reference guide instead of knowing God and living in the truth of his revelation. In light of that, my qualms with evolution were just a drop in the primordial ooze.

I still had a lot to learn about how to interpret the Bible and how to discuss theology with fellow Christians. The woman who taught my Sunday school class helped lead to my next shift in understanding the Bible.

Paul Was a Sexist?

While I finally accepted that the Bible didn't need to be guarded as the foundation of the Christian faith, I still thought it was simple to interpret provided I stuck with a literal, face-value reading. Any hint of taking cultural context into account felt like that slippery slide into relativism. If the Bible said, "don't do this," then it made sense simply to trust and obey the teaching of Scripture.

Unfortunately, interpreting Scripture isn't so cut and dry. Besides regulating—not outlawing—polygamy and slavery, two practices outlawed in most nations today, the Bible also provides rather unusual commands, such as regulations for head coverings and the length of one's hair. Then we need to figure out what to do with the Old Testament laws regarding sacrifices, purity, and worship. We obey some and not others. As a literalist, I thought these were simply self-evident matters, even though I wouldn't have much to say if pressed to divulge a method of interpretation. Wasn't it enough to rely on common sense?

By overlooking the complexity of the Bible, I made at least two mistakes. First of all, I didn't deal with the Bible's ambiguity. Secondly, by simplifying the Bible, I ignored key portions, especially the parts that I found disagreeable. For example, I rarely ever considered how salvation by faith gelled with the rather frightening story of the sheep and the goats in Matthew 25:31-46. In that passage, it seems that judgment is based on works, a matter that threw a wrench in my understanding of salvation by faith and not by works. However, what really mangled my neat little interpretive grid was allowing women to teach in church.

It seemed that Paul had outlawed women as teachers, not allowing them to speak in meetings, let alone hold positions of authority over men (1 Tim 2:12). I didn't think there was a lot to interpret. The matter seemed clear. For whatever reason, Paul put an end to any prospect of women teaching in the church, and that settled it.

But then I began attending a Sunday school class for college students taught by a woman. I didn't even think about it at first. She was our teacher, and that was that. It was also the most powerful Sunday school class in which I've ever been involved. She didn't merely teach, but dynamically lived out her faith, closing the Bible after our study time so we could pray and practice what we read. Who would have thought you could wake up enough to truly experience God in Sunday school?

Though my understanding of women in ministry developed and evolved into an egalitarian view where women are equals before God both in creation (Gen 1:27) and in ministry, that Sunday school class introduced me to the complexities of interpreting the Bible. While I could dig up verses in Scripture that seemed to outlaw the involvement of women as teachers, I could also find verses that affirmed women as both leaders and teachers. God didn't seem to have any issues with Deborah as a judge over Israel, it didn't seem out of the ordinary for the king of Judah and the priests to seek the counsel of a female prophet in matters of religion (2 Kgs 22:14-20), and even Paul—the guy who was supposed to be against women leading or teaching—mentioned the apostle Junia at the end of his epistle to the Romans.

So which part of the Bible is correct? Was God out of male candidates for judges, leaving Deborah as the only remaining option? Did Josiah misstep by consulting a female prophet, even if she faithfully passed on a message from the Lord? Did Paul intend to say something different about Junia? And if God didn't seem to mind women leading or teaching men, what in the world was Paul thinking when he wrote to Timothy?

I continued to explore these issues in seminary, and I read many books and articles that articulated the issues at hand. However I sliced it, one part of the Bible could not be read as "literally" as I'd always thought possible. Something had to give.

In the end, I concluded that women are approved by God to lead and to teach for a host of reasons. Culturally speaking, it is now conceivable for women to hold leadership positions in government, businesses, and educational institutions. Also, I have seen many effective women ministers who, in my judgment, served in the power of the Holy Spirit. And speaking of the Holy Spirit, I read how many Christians felt a conviction from the Holy Spirit that there is neither "male nor female" in Christ Jesus (Gal 3:28)—an interpretive stretch according to some scholars, but an important point that helped me come to the same conclusion as I read 1 Timothy and studied its context. From what I could see the Holy Spirit doing all around me and in the examples of Huldah and Deborah, there was no reason to doubt that men and women, both made in God's image, have equal roles to play in ministry.

As I settled into my new interpretation on women in ministry, I saw a need not only to rethink the Bible as my foundation, but how I interpreted the Bible in my daily study. While I still practiced Bible study, I'd also glimpsed the role of the Holy Spirit—something I'd rarely considered back in high school and throughout most of college. While the Bible still carries authority and guides our theology, I began to see that the Holy Spirit continues to lead us in our interpretations. The voice of the Spirit keeps our hearts from hardening as we read Scripture and look to God to transform us into a holy people. While we cannot afford to ignore the Holy Spirit as we read Scripture, the possibility that we might requires careful steps forward.

After changing my views on women in ministry, I felt like I was about to open Pandora's box. If I could wiggle around these restrictions on women, wasn't I undermining the authority of the Bible and opening the door for all manner of interpretations that matched my preferences? This is a hard question that cannot be waved away in a chapter or even a book. We have layers and layers of issues to work through when it comes to interpreting the Bible. If there's one thing I know for sure, it's that reading the Bible is no longer as simple as I once thought. While interpreting the Bible is not hopeless, it requires the intervention of God through the person of the Holy Spirit. In responding to the Holy Spirit, under the guidance of Christian traditions and communities, I have found a solid footing for Bible study.

A Spirit-Response Reading of Scripture

If we ask ourselves what we bring to the Bible before we open its pages, we begin Bible study with two key questions. I'm sure every Baptist uses a study Bible or some kind of tool to answer the first question: "What did this mean for the original audience?" However, we must ask another essential question: "What is God's Spirit saying to us today?" In other words, we are not simply amassing a foundation of truth when we read the Bible, but listening to God's Spirit as we study these inspired writings. We can't twist the Bible to say whatever we want because we not only work to uncover its original literary/historical meaning, but also the meaning God's Spirit gives to the Bible as we read it today.

If we believe the Holy Spirit inspired the Scriptures, then it isn't too far of a stretch to take Jesus at his word that this same Spirit will also lead us to the truth and bring about the life of God. In reading the Bible, I've learned that I'm not only trying to understand what it means, but I'm also looking for the leading of the Holy Spirit. Each time I return to the Bible, the Spirit responds with different teachings, meanings, and applications. This is a delicate balance where I approach the Bible as a reader and will surely take something away from what I read, but I also listen for God's Spirit to continue speaking through the words of Scripture, sharing the message of God's reality, the truth that will set us free. I like to call this continual listening to the Holy Spirit a "Spirit-response" approach to Scripture. At the end of the day, it is God's meaning, God's message, that will speak into our lives, spiritually revamping us into God's people who not only understand God's story, but who also live it out. The freedom and abundant life spoken of in Scripture becomes more than a good story. It becomes our new reality as we allow the Spirit to respond to the Bible.

This does not entitle us to a supposed Holy Spirit-led free-for-all whenever we read the Bible. We are not making all interpretations relative. Unlike reader-response criticism that emphasizes the interpretations of the reader over the original intent of the author, we look to the Holy Spirit, the original author, to guide us to the truth. When we look to the Spirit, we are not elevating our own reading, but rather expecting to hear from the Spirit. With these ideals in mind, we should never make sweeping theological decisions based merely on our own sense of the Spirit's leading. That is where our traditions and Christian communities provide guidance. Have Christians throughout history come to similar conclusions? Can your friends affirm that God is leading you in a particular direction? Can you find other passages of Scripture that line up with your views? As we listen to the voice of God's Spirit through Scripture, we also open ourselves up to the Spirit's work through Christians who have gone before us and who walk with us.

I used to be skeptical of people who claimed to interpret Scripture through the guidance of the Holy Spirit. It struck me as a cover for Christians who simply wanted to manipulate the Bible to say what they wanted. However, by the grace of God I've learned that God's Spirit is at work in my own reading of Scripture, bringing knowledge, peace, and renewal. In my struggles with anxiety, I have seen the Holy Spirit use the truth of Scripture to unleash the freedom of God's kingdom into my life.

I can't explain my struggles with anxiety any better than that I became disturbingly aware of my breathing and felt I needed to regulate each breath, deliberately breathing in and out lest I pass out from lack of air. I began to panic and went to the hospital. My mind raced and my heart pumped as I sucked air in and pushed it out amidst the seeming tranquility of the emergency room. Everyone sat quietly while I gasped for air. I went up to the receptionist and pleaded, "I really need help. I'm having trouble breathing, and I don't know what to do!"

A nurse walked over and explained, "You're hyperventilating. You just need to sit down, try to relax, and even hold your breath for a little while to settle down."

It helped to have an inkling of what was happening, and so I sat down as prescribed and did my best to remain calm. I was soon ushered into an examination room where they found nothing wrong with me. In the following months, I was X-rayed, CAT-scanned, and tested for ailments in my heart and lungs. Nothing showed up.

I wrote it off as allergies for a few years. However, I often grew short of breath on the way in to work, when my wife and I had an argument, or when I anticipated some other kind of conflict with people. It sometimes happened when I checked my e-mail or voicemail, and curiously subsided when I didn't find any angry messages. I couldn't or wouldn't connect the dots.

Everything came to a head during a family vacation at Lake George. My wife's cousin and his wife sat on the dock with us. We were about two feet above the water, and their one-year-old son scrambled all over the dock. I almost couldn't bear to watch him as I gasped for breath.

It finally clicked.

While sitting on the dock, I realized that I had an anxiety problem, and I needed prayer. A few hours later, I spilled my guts to my wife and in-laws. We immediately set to praying, and it was like I'd been waiting all my life to cry about this, as if pain, terror, and fear were backed up in my mind, just waiting to be flushed out. I sobbed and sobbed while they prayed for God to remove fear and anxiety, claiming the promise of freedom in Christ from the powers of this world: "So if the Son sets you free, you will be free indeed" (John 8:36).

In that moment, I took a step toward trusting that the teachings of the Bible could be true in fresh, powerful ways in my life.

Without any prompting, a verse from 2 Timothy 1:7 took over my thoughts: "For God did not give us a spirit of timidity, but a spirit of power, of love, and of self-discipline." It felt like a stretch of an application, but as I prayed through that passage, I realized that God does not hand out fear. Fear is something that God works to eradicate. Therefore, as a child of God I didn't have to accept fear in my life, but asked God to replace it with faith, allowing me to rest in his power. In that moment I had an irresistible sense that I was living in the kingdom of God; that I had crossed into a new realm. The freedom of that moment revolutionized my life.

While I still struggle occasionally with anxiety, during that afternoon at Lake George the power of anxiety and fear was broken in my life. I have been resting in God's promise never to give us a spirit of fear, but to give us his power to overcome. That simple verse of Scripture, which I can't remember reading at any one time, was simply sown into my mind. At the right moment, God's Spirit caused it to sprout, and now it is firmly rooted in my life. I can always draw on that life-giving truth from Scripture. It also serves as a reminder to read Scripture continually, always planting the seeds of

God's truth into my mind, waiting for the Spirit to bring about the life of God.

The Bible surely tells us what to believe, but it also tells us how we should live. If we want to see the freedom and life promised in Scripture flow into our lives, we need to read Scripture looking for more than meaning; we need to look for the direction of the Holy Spirit. A friend of mine, who knows the Bible forward and backward, says he rarely puts the Bible down until he senses the Holy Spirit has spoken into his life. While there's nothing wrong with Bible studies that flesh out historical settings or context, we shouldn't pass on an opportunity to hear from the Holy Spirit. This means the Spirit does the interpreting for us, which is something I find comforting in a world that calls our objectivity into question. Instead of worrying about the limitations we bring to our readings of Scripture, we can ask the Spirit to guide us—always leaving ourselves open to a Spirit-response reading of Scripture.

Interpreting the Bible is a lifelong process that is never quite finished. Over time, my understanding of the centrality of the Holy Spirit for Bible study shifted and took different forms. Some may even call the study of Scripture a journey—not that I would.

LOST AND FOUND

Some Christians talk about "journeys" or "trudging along a path" or other traveling metaphors when speaking of their spiritual growth. The metaphor can be a cliché, but there's another reason I choose not to think of myself as a "traveler" on a Christian "journey." For me, it sounds too neat and simple and compares the Christian life to a trip from point A to point B. I prefer to think of the Christian life, and understanding the Bible for that matter, as being lost in the right direction.

We're generally taking steps here and there toward God, but we're all so damaged and imperfect that we take frequent wrong turns, crash, go in circles, and wind up at dead ends. And yet mercifully, we are never lost. That is grace, lavish grace, that saves us from pulling over. To be sure, we're going toward God, but to call it a journey seems too stylized in my view. We make stupid, grievous, bone-headed mistakes, and still find our way back to the freedom, joy, and love of God.

Looking back at the ways I've understood and used the Bible, I can see that I have been simultaneously lost and found at the same time. While the

Bible has been the word of life and truth, I have used it to condemn, bind, and wound. It has been sweet at times, even if I've managed to make it bitter.

Then, by the grace of God, I have stumbled onto the lavish, ridiculously generous promise of Jesus to send the Holy Spirit to guide us into the truth, to lead us on our way. God is truly with us. We have not been left as orphans. Rather, we live in the care of the Holy Spirit who teaches us from Scripture, saving us from the folly of using it as a weapon against fellow believers or even as a foundation for our faith. The Holy Spirit reminds us that we have a relationship with the triune God, and the Holy Spirit uses the Bible to keep us living for God. For all the times when we are lost, it is a comfort to know God has made his home among us.

Chapter 3

RE-IMAGINING THE BATH

Michael Raimer-Goodman

It has been twenty years since the first time I shed my old skin, clothes, and shoes, but I still remember it being a big deal for my family, my church, and myself. Though it was officially my first death and resurrection, it was one of many more to come.

My aunt cancelled her Sunday morning responsibilities at another church in order to attend, and I got to spend the following week at my grandmother's beautiful and enchanting Appalachian home. My mom starting holding me accountable to a different type of behavior than she did before that ceremonious occasion. She would say, "Well, son, now that you're a Christian . . . ," and proceed with some standard or another that I didn't realize I had agreed to live by. It was as though, unbeknownst to me at the time, I had signed up not only to die to various unpleasantries—sin, hell, separation from God, etc.—but also to live toward something that I still had not figured out. It was also as though this new "something" toward which I was supposed to live could be summed up in a list of do's and don'ts.

My church encouraged my wintering process, whereby the leaves of my former self fell to the decaying pile below, but it did not always provide a clear image of what the new leaves might look like once the spring of my new life had sprung. Perhaps the most my six-year-old self could take in was that baptism was a confession of a seemingly infinite string of sinful and disobedient acts that keep us separated from God and an initiation into a life of following the dictates of God usually passed down by older people, but especially by parents. In my pre-baptismal interview with my children's minister, I certainly did not get what the difference was between the old rules and the new rules—the difference between my old leaves, skin, clothes, and shoes, and the new ones I decided to wear.

As I became older, and more adjusted to the new rules—no smoking, no drinking, no cursing, no having premarital sex, no working on Sunday unless you had no other option, no spending time with people who could "corrupt" you, no questioning the authority of Scripture, the usual sort for a Southern Baptist evangelical—I began to wonder about the difference between following those rules and following the rules I denounced with my baptism. Was there a reason why we had this set of obligations and not a different set, not just about how to act, but also about what to think? For example, why didn't our rules in the church say no eating fatty foods, instead of no smoking? Or, why didn't we worry more about helping people who had few clothes than about buying new fancy clothes for Sunday church? Or, instead of saying we must understand Scripture as infallible, why wasn't the rule that we must wrestle intensely with the meaning of Scripture, using any and all help to illuminate God's word? Why do we avoid discussions of money in the church and spend more time on issues we have no record of Jesus mentioning—homosexual orientation, gambling, Christian vs. non-Christian music, and the like? Why do we feel the need to identify Christianity with the history of our nation and culture, knowing the great number of lives that were exploited to create our nation (native peoples, African/African Americans, indentured servants from all over the globe, our widespread use of sweatshops in developing countries to feed our culture's voracious consumerism)?

These questions about the heart of the laws that structure our communities—where they come from, how they are connected, why they have validity, etc.—began to trouble me. It wasn't so much that I felt like I needed to run out and go smoking, drinking, and sexing up all the time, but rather that my inherited faith said it was important to avoid certain behaviors and pressed me only to believe a given script about who God, Jesus, Scripture, etc. was in order to be right with God. Some part of me simply wanted to shed the burden of maintaining a checklist of what to do, what not to do, and what to believe, but I hadn't learned any option other than following a set of do's and don'ts. I felt suffocated by them, but did not know how to find the nearest oxygen tank. I still felt like a naked winterized tree, anticipating the creation of new leaves but not knowing from whence they would come. As I began studying the Gospel accounts of Jesus, I found an answer much different from my church's notion of the bloody Jesus whose main purpose was to help us follow certain rules and doctrines and help us play the games of church.

I saw in Jesus a heroic figure who not only made a significant splash in history, but who also angered a lot of people. On multiple occasions, Jesus is recorded as having broken a particular rule that religious leaders thought he should keep, and ultimately this landed him on the cross. On multiple occasions, Jesus challenged the status quo and pointed toward a new in-breaking reality that he called the kingdom of God. I was mystified, and still am mystified, by what held Jesus so captivated, so dedicated to a task that he would embrace death for it.

Whether it was believing in God's intimate relationship with himself, believing that sinners such as Zacchaeus, prostitutes, unclean lepers, and madmen also had a place at God's table, or believing that one could rightfully work on a Sabbath if it served humanity, Jesus constantly placed himself at odds with those charged with keeping order in his society. Either this was the work of a destructive rebel, hell-bent on knocking down his own social order, or it was the work of someone with a radically different vision of what the world could and should be.

In Matthew 12:24, the religious leaders, whose duty was to oversee social and religious order, charge Jesus with working in the name of Beelzebub, the prince of demons. So convinced are they that Jesus is working against the ordained rules of God that they charge him with playing for the other team—the one that wrecks havoc, destroys life, promotes lies, and hates God. This is a serious charge, rooted in the radical and foreign nature of Jesus' actions and the corresponding spiritual dullness of the judgment-passing religious and social leaders.

Jesus shed some things, soundly dispatching them as non-determinative for his life and vision, but unlike me, he lived with new skin, clothes, and shoes. The new leaves on the spring he ushers in were finally made visible to me. In Luke 10:25, a lawyer asks Jesus to describe the heart of these new leaves: "Teacher, what must I do to inherit eternal life?" Jesus asks the lawyer to offer his interpretation of the law. The lawyer replies, "Love the Lord your God with all your heart and with all your soul and with all your strength and with all your mind, and your neighbor as yourself." Jesus affirms that this is required for life in his spring by saying, "You have answered correctly; do this and you will live."

The fulfillment of the law and the prophets is the fulfillment of those two laws, and they are fundamentally relational. Luke helps ensure our understanding that Jesus did not think some people are our neighbors, perhaps those with whom we agree on certain theological or political issues or with whom we share a common ethnic history, while other people are not. In Luke, the lawyer presses the issue further, wanting to make sure he is dressed appropriately for the new life, and asks, "Who is my neighbor?" Essentially, this is the same question as "Whom do I have to love as myself, and whom do I not have to love as myself?" It's a common question that most of us ask all the time in one form or another, whether implied in our actions or stated openly.

Jesus turns the question on its head. To demonstrate his point, he tells the story of a man who fell among robbers along a notoriously rough road near Jerusalem, then was beaten and left for dead. Two religious men walk by and, keeping with the custom to avoid unseemly dead people, continue on about their business. A Samaritan, a member of a Hebrew sect despised by Jews at that time for various and in my opinion insignificant historical reasons, acted compassionately toward the beaten man. When asked to identify the neighbor in this story, the lawyer finds that his question has been turned inside out. Instead of the neighbor being someone else, the lawyer is charged with the task of being the neighbor to whoever is in front of him, regardless of the extant differences and similarities.

If the old life is marked by estrangement from God and the ensuing damage done to our neighbors and ourselves, then the new life is marked by loving God with all that we are and embodying this love in our relationships with everyone we see. The critical element for anything worth doing, according to Jesus, is whether it expresses love for God, and for our neighbor as ourselves.

This new life into which I was baptized and into which I continue to seek to be reborn, sounds nice and pleasant enough at first. As one of my heroes Tony Campolo once said in a sermon, if you just talk about love, you don't get put on the cross; you get invited to speak at the Rotary Club. What makes this new law so dangerous is that so much of this world is not founded on love. Much of this world is founded on self-deification, characterized by fear and pride and efforts to turn our neighbors into the means of achieving our own ends. I found this, and still find this, not just in the "world out there" but also in "the world in here"—in the church where I grew up, in my family, in my friends, in myself.

Just as Jesus Christ died as a result of his relentless submission to God, those who answer the call to the new life in Christ also die to our former selves and ways of relating that fall short of God's command to love. While this is represented in the Baptist church in the act of baptism—going under the water—it is reenacted countless times throughout the course of our lives. Every time we encounter a part of us that is not in accord with the love command, Christ invites us to come and die. The hope is that as we die to our former selves, we are reborn into the life of the Spirit whose heart is love.

I remember several times throughout the course of my life in which I have had to come and die. Perhaps the most dramatic of these came not when I was baptized as a six-year-old, but as an adolescent whose self-regard was fairly poor. I had a hard time understanding and accepting my life, my identity, my direction, my purpose, and generally did not relate to myself as a true child of God should. I had the gift of a friend who, along with the rest of his family, accepted and loved me in ways much deeper than I did myself. Confronted with the discrepancy between how he and his family viewed and loved me, that is to say with the love of Christ, and the way I did not love myself, I was called to come and die. If I were to be a disciple of Christ, my way of understanding, relating to, and accepting myself would have to change. I could not love a God who had died for me and not also love myself.

I have come to believe that we cannot truly love ourselves unless we truly love God. We cannot even accept or understand who we are without appreciating the origins of our existence. Likewise, we can never love God without truly loving ourselves, because in devoting our disposition entirely to the God of Jesus Christ, we devote ourselves entirely to the belief that the world and all of its inhabitants were created good. Thus, loving God with all of our heart, soul, strength, and mind is primary in Christ's command to love, but it naturally leads into the second command of loving our neighbors as we love ourselves.

When I have found myself most deeply connected to God in love, I have been able to encounter my neighbor as I would myself—with appreciation of our differences and an awareness that we are deeply connected through the creative work of the God I love. Because I can be open to receiving all of my neighbors as I would myself, and acknowledge the goodness of the life expressed in a different human form than it is in my own, I can delight in our differences and desire for that person the fullest expression of their God-given life. As such, when I love God as completely as I can, diversity becomes an asset and not an enemy. Diversity becomes a doorway to self-exploration as I see myself in my neighbor, and a means to freedom. Because I acknowledge that my neighbor's life is loved and accepted by God because of who God is and not because of the choices my neighbor has made, I realize that I too have the freedom to be different. My neighbor becomes a mirror, under the light of God's grace, to see different potentials in myself that I could not see on my own.

In my life, my commitment to seeing all of my neighbors as siblings created by God and as means to understanding the diverse expressions of the *imago dei* has taken many forms and taught me many lessons. From living with inner-city youth to listening to the stories of residents of the West Bank, from helping refugees who are fleeing war-torn countries to seeing the suffering of God in lives mangled by lack of food in developing countries, from visiting with people who spend their life savings on the hope of gaining a better life in the United States to interacting with people whose lives have been forever changed by senseless acts of violence, I have had the opportunity to see myself in the lives of individuals from many different walks of life. In all of this, I have tried to ask myself, "If I love this person like I love myself, how should I relate to him or her?" This is, after all, the nucleus of the Second Commandment and the means to becoming a neighbor.

In these various relationships, I have found a deeper connection with other people, other children of God, and consequently a deeper understanding of the way my own life could and should be. In many cases, I have found myself on the way to another death and resurrection, another movement in the process initiated by baptism.

I spent one summer in East Saint Louis, Illinois, during the summer following my sophomore year of college. East Saint Louis is one of the poorest urban areas in the nation. While there, I made a friend named Damien McCoy. He was eight years old, with a beautiful smile and an enormous heart. I worried and prayed daily for Damien as I did all of the children in the Christian Activity Center. I was concerned for their safety in a violent subculture. I was concerned for their self-perception because the surrounding communities often ignored and seemed to despise the children and adults who lived in East Saint Louis. This could be seen in a variety of ways. Often church groups came into the center, and rather than sitting with, listening to, and getting to know the children and the issues they face and the strength they find to address these concerns, they would only see a reflection of their own heroism in coming to the city. They would see needy children who required their heroic efforts to be saved. Most church groups that visited the center presented the "gospel," and at the end of these visits the same children responded again to the gospel as if for the first time. The children knew this was how they could receive special treatment for the short period, and few of the church groups knew that the children they had "saved" were the same children who were "saved" the week before. While the church groups assumed that they expressed love for the children, it came off more as a lack of respect and genuine concern for the children. Love must include knowledge and respect in order for it to be real love. Real love of these children would ask the question, "What are the biggest challenges these children will face, and how can I join their efforts to address these challenges?" The pseudo-love that was often expressed sought only to build up the feelings of self-importance from the visiting churches. I worried that these children would receive an image of God that showed only marginal concern about them. Fortunately, I knew many other people who truly loved these children and the community and were committed to representing a God who was radically committed to their entire well-being. These people have died to their own need for self-importance and entered into a genuine love of these neighbors that is mediated by the Spirit.

I worried about the children because their school systems were atrocious; without a well-established tax base, the schools could not always pay for their own books and could never pay competitive teachers' salaries. The state of Illinois decided to redirect the interstate around East Saint Louis so that passersby would not have to face the reality of the city. This also deeply troubled me. In so many ways, the cards were stacked against this community and its children. I was tempted to pity the community and leave it behind as a faded memory after that summer. The reason I cannot is because of Damien. We formed a deep friendship that summer that eventually became more than a friendship. He often asked me to read to him, and I read stories like David and Goliath. One day we went to the corner store to buy snacks and a drink. We came back to the center, sat at a table, and prepared to eat. This beautiful child with far less material resources than I could imagine split all of his food with me, giving me half. Sharing our little meal became an Emmaus experience for me. In his generosity, he gave me half of everything he bought and represented to me the surprising grace of Christ that always has more to give than I can imagine. Our snacks became the body and blood of Jesus, and Damien became not just a friend but someone who mediated the presence of God to me—an image bearer.

One night later in the summer, as I prayed for the children, I had another surprising revelation. I recalled all the troubles I had seen in the children I prayed for, and begged God to reveal to me the presence of Christ in the sorrow and hardship. I remembered children without shoes, without someone to watch and care for them during the day as their mostly single mothers worked, without three healthy meals for the day, and without good schools necessary for economic uplift. I cried out to God, "I know you love these children. At least I believe you do. Why do they have to suffer like this? Why don't you do something?" One night, the image of the children for whom I prayed turned into the fullness of my understanding of Christ, as if God told me, "I am with these children. I feel their suffering, and as you love them you love me."

This was helpful, but I still struggled with how other churches ignored the plight of these children, and I wondered if church life was just a sham. If Christ is with the children of East Saint Louis, why aren't more of Christ's followers there too? My notion that God would do much work apart from his followers died that summer. I entered into a dark time the following semester, still wondering why God doesn't respond to the suffering of the world and in particular East Saint Louis in a more visible way. How could I believe in an all-powerful, all-loving God in light of human suffering?

During my Christmas break following the summer I spent in East Saint Louis, I went to Israel/Palestine to listen to the stories of Palestinians. Their side of the conflict has not been well represented by pro-Israel media in the West, and a contingent of some of my Christian friends was interested in hearing from them. We wanted to express our love for our global neighbors in Palestine by listening to their sufferings due to the Israeli-Palestinian conflict. We heard many stories of people being dragged into the streets in the middle of the night and stripped of their clothes while Israeli military entered their homes in search of "terrorist activities." Many of the people we visited were Christians, and all of their families had lived in that area for longer than Israel had been a country. Some of the homes were shot through with Israeli bullets. We visited people who lived in or near Jenin, West Bank. Earlier in the year, there was a sizeable battle near Jenin, and we visited with some of the people affected by that fight. One man we visited was in an ambulance when it blew up. The Israeli government had granted permission for the ambulance to pass through the battle to pick up wounded soldiers, but some military types destroyed the ambulance anyway. This man had third-degree burns on 82 percent of his body.

As we left his house and continued walking down the street, a man came up from behind and began to yell something in Arabic. Not knowing Arabic, I asked a translator to interpret. He told me that the man was yelling, "Your planes blew up my family. Your planes blew up my family." The man knew we were Americans, and he knew the origins of the planes the Israelis flew overhead to bomb them. I encountered the other side of our nation's militarism and decided that I couldn't claim to love him, or anyone on the receiving end of American-sponsored violence, and still support our nation's violent foreign policies. This neighbor called me to remember the commitment I demonstrated at baptism: death to violence and hatred and resurrection to loving my neighbor as myself.

I still wrestled with the bigger question, "Why isn't God doing something to stop all this suffering?" I was still depressed from the shock to my worldview that I had received in East Saint Louis, and I realized from my visit to Palestine how much deeper the world's suffering goes. It seemed limitless and palpable. I had a real sense that the suffering of the world was oppressing me, and I did not know where to find daylight, where to find freedom. The caravan I traveled with returned to Zababdeh, West Bank, and I journeyed off to be alone. I roamed around the grounds of the Roman Catholic Church there and aimlessly wandered into a shrine to the Virgin Mary. It was there that I received a surprising answer to the question that had plagued me since earlier that summer. As I walked into the shrine, I was praying but also deeply distressed about things I had seen in God's world. I felt an immediate sense of calm come over me, and I knew it would be best if I simply listened. I looked up at Mary, realized that she must be the pattern for myself, and found the answer to the question, "Why isn't God doing something to end suffering?" I realized that just as Mary allowed God to fill her with the Holy Spirit in order to give birth to the kingdom of God, so too God waits on all of us to open ourselves to the Holy Spirit so that we might give birth to the kingdom of God on earth. It is because too few people have committed themselves to God, dying to themselves and asking to be reborn into the Spirit-filled life working to establish the reign of love in this world, that suffering still exists. I felt called to die to myself, to my selfish concerns and preoccupations, and to be reborn again and more fully into the life of the Spirit. I answered, "No." I understood the cost and was too weak to answer, "Yes." But at least I had my answer.

I have been troubled ever since that day by the fact that I said "no," and I've returned to God countless times to say "yes." It has become a regular part of my prayer life to open myself up to God and ask God to help me die so I can live into the ways of Jesus and the Spirit, but I understand the temptation to say "no." I know that the forces we work against are not weak, but rather we struggle with powers and principalities that seek to wreak havoc on human life. In the thought of the apostle Paul, because of the influence of these powers and principalities, the Spirit is the beginning of the salvation process. We must struggle with our salvation, working it out in fear and trembling because sin continues to live inside of us, saying "no" when we are regularly called to remember the baptismal waters and be reborn into a deeper intimacy with the Spirit.

There are many areas of my life where I have tried to answer "yes" to the Spirit's call to love my neighbor as deeply as I love myself, and thereby learn and demonstrate love for God. Having decided to continue living in the United States for the time being, I am faced with a growing number of Spanish-speaking neighbors. In order to love them as I would myself, and show them hospitality that I would desire, I went to Guatemala to learn Spanish. I have formed good friends who know Spanish better than I do and who are able to help me improve my knowledge of the language. I have been able to show hospitality to many Spanish-only neighbors, especially in Houston, Texas, ranging from people I pass in grocery stores to patients I encounter in the hospital as a chaplain. I understand my efforts to learn Spanish to be a way that I can die to my personal comforts and be reborn into deeper intimacy with the Spirit who calls me to love all others as I want to be loved. I understand my efforts to learn Spanish, therefore, as an extension of my baptism into that Spirit—an act represented in the symbol of my baptism at age six.

Other aspects of my life need to die, and I confess that I am not always as diligent about praying to God that those aspects of my life might die so that new growth can come from the power of the risen Lord. These aspects include my habit of over-consuming food while many of the world's poor go hungry, using so much gasoline that harms our environment and provides reason to go to war with oil-rich countries like Iraq, wasting time indulging myself in entertainment that doesn't draw me closer to God or my neighbors, being apathetic to some of the issues around the world and in my city, and the list goes on. I firmly believe that if I seek to make the changes on my own, I attempt to "save myself" in essence. This will merely result in a feeling of self-righteousness, and of bitterness to others who haven't struggled in the ways that I have to "become perfect as God is perfect." However, if in the course of my prayer life I present to God my concerns and ask God to work in my life to help me die to my various addictions, sources of pride, misplaced origins of self-worth, spiritual sloth and laziness, and other things that prevent me from loving all of my neighbors around the world, if I ask God to help me with these things, and to work salvation through the Spirit that calls and equips me to love, then I can truly be saved. While I doubt that perfection is ever possible in this lifetime, Jesus does call us to "be perfect as our heavenly Father is perfect."

In sum, I have tried to articulate my understanding of baptism as an event in a longer process of salvation, characterized as a pattern of death to self and rebirth into the in-breaking, redemptive work of God through the love of Christ. With this understanding, initiation into the Baptist community, baptism, is not the final end of salvation. Church strength should not be evaluated by how many people are dunked in a given month, but by how many people continue the process of death to anything that stands in the way of loving God with all that one is, loving one's neighbor as oneself, and being reborn into the transformative love and movement of the Spirit. It is appropriate and beautiful that formal entry into the Christian community, baptism, is understood as a death to one's isolated existence and rebirth into the healing love of Christ. Throughout the course of Christian discipleship, this event should be remembered, its meaning deepened, and its commitment rehearsed. In this sense, the reality to which baptism points is like yeast that works its way through the flour to uplift, leaven, and expand the life of the bread.

I have tried to understand the event of baptism in my life and its meaning throughout the course of my continuing efforts to follow the way of Jesus. As I struggle to appropriate its meaning, I find that it has the power to render transformation in my relationships with God and other people. I have no doubt that, understood as the bedrock of Christian fellowship, the pattern of death to one's alienated existence and rebirth into the charismatic life of the Spirit has the ability to transform all the members of the church into a true beloved community. This foundation will not only transform the church from isolated individuals into the unified body of Christ, but will also transform everything that the church touches—that is to say, the world.

Chapter 4

EMERGING WORSHIP: A POSTMODERN EXPERIMENT

Mike Gregg

BAPTIST DISTINCTIVENESS AND THE POSTMODERN ERA

Introduction

First off, I'm not a writer. In fact, even though I am an associate pastor in a Baptist church, I don't feel like a minister either. Many of the things I have learned over the years as a Baptist minister are things that are not attractive to postmodern Christians or the postmodern "unchurched." I find myself having to explore closely the postmodern world and determine the current perceptions of a follower of Christ and how to attract postmodern individuals to Christianity. With this in mind, I fancy myself more of an explorer than anything else. I am exploring what the Church (with a big "C") needs to be for the postmodern world; I am exploring if denominations are important; I am exploring if going to one place for worship is desirable or even necessary; I am exploring the importance of the Jesus of my parents and their parents and whether that Jesus is applicable to seekers today. I consider myself an explorer, and in fact, I have come to the conclusion that if I bring my tendencies toward exploration to this new idea of a postmodern church, I might just tap into what it means to be a Christian in a new and uncharted present.

Postmodernity and Baptists

Wikipedia, which is ironically a postmodern web-based modification of a traditional encyclopedia, claims, "The Western European disillusionment induced by World War II largely influenced postmodernism. Postmodernity (beginning after 1970) tends to refer to a cultural, intellectual, or artistic state lacking a clear central hierarchy or organizing principle and embodying extreme complexity, contradiction, ambiguity, diversity, and interconnectedness."[1] This understanding of the current culture is important in understanding the church's role in worship creation. As Generation X (people born 1961–1981) and Millennials, or Generation Y (people born 1982–2001) continue to gain influence in Christianity and worship leadership, the characteristics of worship will be more postmodern.

Worship adapted to a postmodern world is going to become, and might already be, quite messy. The days of flawless performances on Sunday mornings are over as worshipers seek authentic community and shared experiences. The world will continue to be an uncertain place as difficult questions invade sleep and muddle faith. Postmodern worshipers look for opportunities to be themselves in the midst of the messiness of life. This messiness is beautiful, just as art, poetry, and music can be wonderfully disordered. The reality of a postmodern world is that in this new and uncertain time, worship will be beautiful and messy, noisy and silent, autonomous and full of shared community. As Baptists, we might find that we are actually getting back to our roots.

As I have learned more about postmodernity's effects on Christianity, it seems that as Christians become more postmodern, they might also become more Baptist. I might be a little biased because I am Baptist and love being a Baptist. While Baptists have a long history of close community, fellowship, and missions, Baptist churches are also autonomous, and these congregations try to remain separated from other denominational entities. It appears to onlookers as if Baptists are individualistic and exclusionary. Each church can make its own rules and have its own by-laws. Each individual in the church can interpret and understand Scripture in his or her own way. Yet, at the core of Baptist beliefs are community and shared experiences. The resounding phrase of Baptist distinctiveness is the "priesthood of all believers." The phrase does not say the priesthood of *each* believer but of *all* believers, together. Even though Baptist churches are autonomous, they embody close community and a common connectedness.

Another Baptist distinctive that reveals close community is ordinances. The Lord's Supper and baptism are the two ordinances that reveal the communal nature of Baptists. Although each ordinance is a special moment for the individual receiving the sacrament, each is done in community and in loving relationship with the rest of the church. So Baptists have a way of living out the dichotomy and questions of the postmodern era.

How can the Baptist church be autonomous and yet have members that are strongly connected to each other? It is a question that has pushed Baptists to the brink of disintegration, destruction, and disillusionment. Most Baptist churches have joined the ranks of larger denominational movements by forming organizations and conventions in which to stay connected and gain greater resources. Other Baptist churches have tried to hang on to their independence and autonomy only to be plagued with waning membership, dwindling budgets, and loose affiliations. But being Baptist can once again be a badge of both independence and togetherness as postmodern Christians in Baptist churches seek to live into the questions, the messiness of faith, and a postmodern context and culture.

Baptists and the Emergent Movement

What has modern worship brought to the table, and why won't it work in a postmodern world? Worship spaces are overwhelming in size, while worshipers stare at the back of each other's heads, sit on hard pews, and slouch under the weight of unilateral preaching. Silence is often uncomfortable as it reveals chinks in the armor of a perfectly orchestrated service. Yet, in a postmodern culture of technology, globalization, pluralism, overstimulation, overindulgence, and a plethora of questions, a new movement has arisen: the Emergent Church.

The emergent movement took shape as frustrated Christians began to think about how postmodernism affects faith and how to express that faith in a postmodern world. Thus, community, relationships, and the questioning of faith readily define emergent worship in the postmodern landscape. Many Baptists, just like many Christians, have ridden the wave of progress from the 1980s and 1990s only to find that their worship services are perfectly orchestrated shows. The postmodern world is busy, loud, and at times overwhelming. The emergent movement has tried to respond to this noise with its own cacophony of worship techniques including using technology, caring for nature, utilizing more silence, having dialogue, and employing more relational connections.

But the Emergent Movement is one voice in the midst of many worship styles in the postmodern era including conservative, liberal, liturgical, contemporary, and seeker, to name a few. Many of these worship styles existed in the modern era and are still being used in the postmodern era. They are styles and are all expressions of worship. Postmodern worshipers do not necessarily care about the plethora of styles but want worship services to be intentional, experiential, and communal. Can we still be Baptist in this cacophony of postmodern voices? The answer is to reach back into Baptist roots and be who we have always been, a people of shared experiences and close community.

Journey into Postmodern Community

My Church's Postmodern Exploration

With thousands of churches closing their doors every year, it is difficult to imagine what the landscape of the Christian church will look like in fifty years. Will small churches exist, or will they all filter into the mega churches like mercury in a funnel? Will worshipers prefer to stay home on Sundays rather than add another event to their busy schedules? Will most ministers be out of a job in twenty years? Will this trend cause many young seminary students to become teachers, non-profit directors, and possibly give up church work altogether? I ask myself these questions daily. I ask them because my church is slowly decreasing in membership along with many others. And just like other churches, my church has a difficult and slow time adapting to a changing postmodern culture.

My friend, a fellow Generation Xer, told me he didn't like to go to church because he could barely stay awake in Sunday morning worship. He wondered why he should wake up early to sing hymns he does not know, listen to a sermon that does not relate to his life, and leave feeling like he was watching God on a Friday night television drama. God did not feel present to him. His fellow worshipers were not real to him and were merely rows of cardboard cutouts and backs of heads. The only person who could tell if he was not paying attention was the preacher. But the preacher wasn't paying attention because he was too busy listening to his own voice to care about the blank stares and the wandering minds.

With what kind of worship would my postmodern peer connect? Like my friend, I am a Generation Xer. I am close enough to the back side of Generation X almost to be a Millennial, so I am extremely postmodern in my approach to worship styles. Yet I minister in a traditional Baptist church with a liturgical worship service from the modern era. The difference between my friend and me is that I have had seminary training and have learned how to sense the presence of the Spirit and to worship God in all contexts and styles. My friend, though, wasn't sure how to approach God and experience Jesus outside of a postmodern context. It became apparent that my church needed a postmodern worship service with emergent characteristics. This new service would move beyond the praise bands, video screens, and personalities of the still widely popular modern and contemporary church. This new worship gathering would meet postmoderns where they are and attend to their need for a relevant and shared experience of God.

Church 101: A Postmodern Worship Experience

This is a general outline for the postmodern worship service at our church:

Sharing of Food
We build relationships through the fellowship of food.

Transition of Moods
The lighting of a candle, the pouring of water, the movement of sand, the reading of poetry, or the playing of music help worshipers transition from the informal lunch to the sacred Communion.

Communion
The Lord's Supper consists of variations in implementation and styles such as giving Communion to each other, using different elements for the bread and wine based on the theme of the service, and employing different liturgy in presenting the bread and cup.

Silence
Long periods of silence are important for self-reflection and spiritual focus.

Prayer
Prayer is guided through litanies, poetry, centering prayer, intercessory visioning, movement, call and response, and chanting.

Dialogical Sermons
Worshipers' questions and interests determine the topics of sermons. A facilitator presents information regarding the topic and then guides the group conversation.

Discussion

Small group discussion might extend the conversation on the sermon.

Music

Musicians play instruments of all types; CDs with contemporary songs reveal the themes of the sermons; songs and hymns are sung as a group.

Many churches have aging congregations and thus a sparse population of Generation Xers or Millennials to share ideas and visions. In order to glean the postmodern personality for worship, I enlisted the help of my church's seminary interns to help me imagine an alternative worship service designed for postmoderns. All three interns are younger than twenty-six years old; two are female and one is male. Although the interns (and I) are white and middle-class, we all have experience with people of different cultures, ages, and socioeconomic levels. The interns and I met to form a plan of action. We had not done much research in the emergent church movement, but our ideas leaned toward that model based on our life experiences and desire for a more casual and postmodern-centered worship.

Several issues facing the church—the lack of both money and volunteers—guided our planning as we tried to design this new worship experience. First, we wanted to implement a worship experience that would incur little to no expense because a struggling economy and dwindling church attendance left little money for new ventures. We decided we would gather together every second and fourth Sunday until the worship service became popular enough to support itself monetarily. Second, we wanted to rotate our leadership so that one person would not be the main figurehead and organizer of the service. Thus, volunteers have less stress as responsibilities are divided.

Our planning of a new worship service needed to include characteristics of the postmodern community. First, we wanted to tap into a postmodern worshiper's need to have relationships and experience God in settings different from a formal sanctuary. Many postmoderns feel more comfortable in a bar, coffeehouse, home, or movie theater. In order to mimic the need for varying and comfortable locations, we sought to use the church's spacious building. Due to limited church events and decreasing membership, many of the gathering places in the church building are used seldom or not at all. These spaces included the sanctuary, the smaller chapel, the fellowship hall, the baseball field, the newly renovated youth area, and an amphitheater.

These spaces could lead to unique worship experiences not found in the sanctuary on Sunday mornings.

Second, we needed to find a time that was convenient for postmodern worshipers. Young adults of the Generation X and especially Generation Y communities work hard and play even harder. They have high expectations of themselves and work hard to prove it, not only to themselves but to people around them as well. When the weekend comes, they party, play, and relax with intensity. Activities and worship services on Sunday morning, especially Sunday school at 9:00 or 9:30 A.M., are extremely early for postmodern adults who have played hard the night before. It seems that many postmoderns begin to move and get started on their day around lunchtime. We decided that this time appeared appropriate for a postmodern worship service. We chose 1:00 P.M. as our start time.

As the interns and I continued to plan, we recognized that this new worship service was not only novel for the church but also a completely new way for some people to worship. It seemed fitting that the beginning time for this new worship service should change from 1:00 P.M. to 1:01 P.M. This one-minute change signified that we would learn how to do church all over again, together. We were going back to basics. We were in essence taking a class called Church 101. This new time made our worship service seem less threatening, easy to grasp for churched and non-churched alike, and gave a clear designation as to the beginning time of the service each Sunday.

As the skeleton of Church 101 was formed, we wanted to flesh out what it meant to be a part of the Church 101 community and the importance of sharing our lives, our hurts and joys, our difficulties and achievements, our anger and our happiness. This is what the disciples did with Jesus, and it is what we wanted to do with those worshipers who gathered for Church 101. The natural Scripture to which the interns and I were drawn was Mark 14:22-26:

> While they were eating, Jesus took bread, gave thanks and broke it, and gave it to his disciples, saying, "Take it; this is my body." Then he took the cup, gave thanks and offered it to them, and they all drank from it. "This is my blood of the covenant, which is poured out for many," he said to them. "I tell you the truth, I will not drink again of the fruit of the vine until that day when I drink it anew in the kingdom of God." When they had sung a hymn, they went out to the Mount of Olives.

This appeared to be the perfect outline for our postmodern worship service: the fellowship of food, the sharing of Communion, the importance of contemplation, the soul-satisfying sound of music, and the going out to encounter Christ, in all Christ's glory and hurting, in the world.

A Place of Sharing

As the seminary interns and I dwelled upon and contemplated this biblical text, we were attracted to the notion that shared lives and a shared experience is an important aspect of postmodern worship. Church 101 would understand worship as being a place of shared responsibilities, shared food, and shared discussion.

First, Church 101 seeks to have shared responsibilities. A prominent notion in the emergent church movement is humility. A big voice and a big personality on a big stage is a representation of the modern age of church worship. Many mega churches have a dynamic preaching personality upon which the entire church is built. Granted, many mega churches have small groups of faithful and well-connected members. In the postmodern age of Christian worship, worship attendees are beginning to realize a broader experience than the one that can come from a solitary voice. The days of a CEO pastor are dwindling as postmoderns seek to get involved and get their hands dirty in social service, worship planning and implementation, and caring for one another. Many people are burned out with the expectations of their jobs, families, homes, and extracurricular activities and cannot give their time as freely to the church as in the past. So shared responsibilities in the church and in worship help diffuse some of the anxiety that arises in an overworked postmodern society. However, ease of implementation is not the only reward from shared responsibilities. Different voices in worship planning add multiple personalities, cultures, and ideas to the worship experience and to the work of the church in the world. Christianity begins to be less like one pastor and more like the members of the church and the people of a postmodern world.

Second, our new worship service allows worshipers to share food with one another. The logistics of having lunch after the traditional worship service was complicated due to the meager funds to buy food and the limited personnel to prepare it. In classic Baptist fashion, many in our church believed that we had to have a huge, home-cooked meal any time we shared food together. However, our church's limited resources and cooks made this a daunting task. Our first service, the traditional worship service, begins at

11:00 A.M. and finishes at noon or later. The volunteers to cook the meal would have to miss the 11:00 A.M. service in order to prepare lunch and be finished before the postmodern worship began at 1:01 P.M. Also, our church is a commuter church, and many members come from all parts of Atlanta to worship together. Many do not have time to come back to church on a different day for committee meetings, gatherings, and classes. Most church committee meetings are scheduled directly after the first service at noon and usually finish at 1:00 P.M., so committee members don't get too cranky from missing lunch. The logistics of having Church 101 begin at 1:01 P.M. would mean that members with meetings after the first traditional service could not attend the postmodern service. Asking members to go to committee meetings after church was difficult, but we knew that asking them to miss lunch in order to attend yet another service is irresponsible leadership. How were we going to fill stomachs so that we could, in turn, feed spirits?

As mentioned earlier, the Lord's Supper narrative of Mark held particular significance for us as we planned Church 101. This notion of food as worship has been important throughout time not only for Christians in general but for Baptists as well. I would wager that every Baptist has several memories of growing up in the church and enjoying potluck lunches, church-wide picnics, and "dinner on the grounds." In fact, Baptists might have a better recollection of the different types of casseroles brought to a church lunch than they do of a sermon topic on any particular Sunday. Food is important for Baptists and a key form of fellowship for Christians throughout time. It was an easy decision when one of the interns suggested, "Why don't we make lunch a part of the worship service instead of something we do before it?" The first verse of Mark's Lord's Supper narrative says, "*While they were eating* [my emphasis], Jesus took bread, gave thanks and broke it, and gave it to his disciples." Jesus transitioned from the fellowship and communion of food to the worship and communion of the first Lord's Supper and remembering of Jesus.

The separation of eating supper for physical sustenance and sharing in this new institution of the Lord's Supper for spiritual sustenance was not found in the Bible. There seemed to be a seamless transition from one to the other. This physical to spiritual transition is what we hoped to accomplish in Church 101. Lunch, made of easy-to-prepare meals like sandwiches, soup, and salads, brings worshipers together to share their lives—and a meal—in informal fellowship. Then, when all worshipers have their fill and are satisfied, we transition directly into the Lord's Supper. This brings the worshipers' focus from their own physical bodies to the physical body of Jesus and how Jesus nourishes our spiritual selves. The style and texture of the Lord's Supper might change week to week in accordance with the theme of the day and the diversity of ways to partake in Communion. One Sunday, the Lord's Supper might consist of raisin bread and white grape juice as we focus on the sweetness of the Spirit. Another day, worshipers might use real wine and a non-alcoholic substitute in order to practice the ritual of Intinction. And yet another Lord's Supper might be saltine crackers and apple juice to help us remember the childlike faith with which we all come to Jesus. So the Lord's Supper becomes a transition point from the fellowship and nourishment of our physical selves to the beginning of worship and the fellowship and nourishment of our spiritual bodies.

Third, shared Communion leads worshipers into shared discussion. A classic sermon is not preached in Church 101. The leader for the day guides worshipers into a biblical text, a social concern, an emotional conundrum, or a faith question. The worshipers tell us during the first gathering of Church 101 what they struggle with and the items of faith that give them pause. If some worshipers are not present or do not feel comfortable testifying to their faith questions, they can submit questions anonymously online through the church website. The facilitators then take those questions and concerns and prepare outlines to guide worshipers into these items. Although a leader provides insight into the suggestions made by worshipers, the facilitator actually helps attendees contemplate the faith questions and work through them with their fellow worshipers. The experiences of everyone in the room are far more valuable than the limited insight of the facilitator. The time of teaching becomes dialogical instead of a monologue by a pastor. Everyone has the authority to come to God and one another with their questions instead of those questions becoming unanswered cancers that eat away at a seeker's life and soul.

The environment of worship can lead to openness in dialogue and community. This environment can be based in the way a worship space is laid out or in the design of the service. Most traditional worship spaces have pews lined front to back with the focus of attention on the backs of each other's heads and centered at a raised stage and pulpit. The only interaction of worshipers with each other is the occasional overhearing of their singing voices with the hymns and possibly a time to "pass the peace." However, if a passing of the peace is not a part of the worship service, then hardly any interaction of worshipers is encountered. Many Christians accustomed to modern American worship value individuality and silence. It is a time of reverent self-reflection and contemplation. The silence is important in a chaotic and busy world. Yet, this is just a piece of what postmoderns need to understand God. God not only comes in the silence, but also in the power of relationships and dialogue.

Many postmoderns do not need to attend a church to understand the power of God in their lives and in the world. They could come to a church building only once a month and feel that they have done their worship duties. Postmoderns are connected through technology and online communities like Facebook as well as cell communities that meet in homes, bars, or coffeehouses. A single place of worship is no longer sacred. Yet, Church 101 seeks to keep postmoderns connected to a church building while appealing to a sense of change and a small-group atmosphere. Church 101 can meet in spaces that are traditional, contemporary, informal, and formal. If the theme of the service has to do with the stewardship of the earth, then worshipers can meet in an amphitheater outside. If more roundtable discussions are needed, they will meet in a fellowship hall or conference room. If the theme is more sacred and has a Taizé style, a smaller chapel with chairs instead of pews is helpful.[2] The space of worship is important to the amount of shared dialogue that can happen.

Conclusion

The landscape of the Church is indeed changing in an increasingly postmodern world. As our culture becomes more ambiguous, diverse, and interconnected, it is important that Christianity continues to find a way to reach out to individuals of a postmodern mindset. Baptists can, and should, be at the forefront of this spiritual, programmatic, and theological shift. But it will be difficult, and it will take time. Many churches need to continue to offer modern services of traditional, contemporary, seeker, and liturgical styles to meet the needs of the Baby Boomer generation and older (1960 and before), as well as worshipers of all ages who connect to God through this type of worship experience. Yet, even as the modern era fades, the postmodern era of Christianity will eventually become a waning movement and a new cultural context will be the impetus to reach out to future worshipers. This is why I am an explorer above anything else, because without a desire to seek and find something new, the world might one day leave Christianity behind. As a Baptist and a Christian, I hope that day never comes.

Notes

1. Wikipedia, "Postmodernism: Reaction to Modernism," http://en.wikipedia.org/wiki/Postmodernism. Accessed 24 January 2010.

2. The Taizé Community is an ecumenical monastic community whose worship includes chants, icons, meditations, and Scripture readings. Taizé worship centers more on prayer and music rather than preaching—in a traditional Protestant sense.

Chapter 5

GIVE US EARS TO HEAR

Wanda Kidd

A CHURCH CONVERSATION

Not long ago I was asked to be on a panel at a traditional First Baptist Church in a small southern town. The topic was the Emergent Church phenomenon. My role was to speak to the trends that I saw in college ministry and to try to interpret how this new way of thinking affects the local congregation. Four of us sat on the small stage: the pastor, who facilitated the event; the associate pastor, who had served on staff for fifteen years; a recent college graduate from a Baptist college who had done her senior thesis on emergent church issues and trends; and me, a consultant for collegiate ministry with a statewide Baptist group.

The audience was made up of a variety of ages and perspectives. It was the second in a series of three sessions hosted by this church to look at some of the issues facing mainline churches. In many ways, the fact that the church offered this opportunity for their congregation was proactive because these conversations have been slow to take place in the southern part of the United States. Long known as the Bible Belt, this area of the South has been resistant to confronting what is happening to the rest of the country in relation to declining interest in organized religion. We have been slow in looking at the issues because we have continued to meet our church budgets, hire multiple staff, take youth groups to camp, and put an army of people on the ground in a matter of hours to help feed, clean, and rebuild in the face of a natural disaster.

Eventually, however, we must notice that even in the last bastion of sacred church tradition, the Sunday morning congregational makeup is largely senior adult, and the age disparity appears to grow wider each week. There is evidence that the exodus begins with high school students and continues until at least their late twenties, but more often than not, it lasts until they are in their thirties. If they return to church at all, they are usually motivated by their children reaching the traditional Sunday school ages of three and four. However, that trend is only applicable to young people who have been reared in the church, and that population has diminished steadily for the last forty years. Eventually, people in the pews have begun to acknowledge that something is different, and that they must take action. If not, everything they have known and grown will vanish. That is a sad and terrifying thought to most of the people who have built and maintained the religious monolith, their spiritual and social mainstay throughout their lives and the lives of previous generations.

These realities and emotions were alive and present in our group that summer evening. There was skepticism on the part of young people who came longing for something I am not even sure they had words to express. I believe they were there because they ached to resolve the dissonance they felt within themselves about their faith; they desired to stay connected to the church of their parents and grandparents and yearned to feel something personal and vibrant in their relationship with Christ. Also present that evening were frustrated senior adults who wanted to know how these young people could resolve their issues and move on. Alongside those who asked "how" were grandparents who wanted to stay connected to their grandchildren but had no language to talk to them about issues of faith.

People caught between rounded out the group. They were both children of the frustrated senior adults and parents of the estranged younger generation and were simply trying to figure out how to survive in this tumultuous time of transition. For them the mantra of life was "Whatever makes you happy," and the stressful truth was that no one was happy.

The dialogue was predictable. We talked about worship styles and postmodernism. Some asked questions about how to grow the church and attract young people to come to church. Some wondered why other churches were growing and they were not. I have been present for many such conversations in the past decade, but as this conversation came to a close, an interchange caught my attention. A lovely older man who was obviously a respected member of the congregation stood to speak. He put his hands in his pockets, and I saw the people adjust in their seats, preparing for what he had to say. He mentioned that when he was in Florida during WWII, he attended First Baptist Church and walked the aisle at the end of his first service there because that is what his church covenant told him to do. He said the people were welcoming and loving, and he knew he had found a safe place to form community while he was stationed there for three months. Furthermore (I paraphrase here), he could not understand why the youth of today did not simply join a church, invest their lives, and move along.

Many thoughts and emotions washed over me as I listened. There was a strong, fragrant memory of that reality of trust during my childhood and youth in church, but I immediately juxtaposed that memory with the rending of trust during my middle years in church. I wanted to weep as I listened to Mr. Billy speak of his understanding of church and then watched the faces of the young people in the audience who knew little to nothing of that reality in their lives. While I sat in my nostalgic haze, a voice beside me cut to the reality of the unvarnished issue of the evening.

The associate pastor, who had a respectful and honest relationship with this older man, said, "It is wonderful that you had that experience, Billy, but I don't hear that you truly want to have a conversation with young people. What I hear is that you will listen to them so that you can tell them why they are wrong and how they should feel about the church, and until they feel the way that you do, they will continue to be wrong." He continued by saying that this was not conversation and that nothing would be changed, solved, or moved forward until ideas like Mr. Billy's changed.

I was stunned. For one thing, I was impressed that a person in leadership courageously and respectfully verbalized a deep conviction in a public forum to the person with whom he disagreed. I was equally delighted with the elder gentleman's gracious acceptance of the differing opinion. My second thought was a sense of grief that this was such a rare occurrence. Immediately on the heels of that thought was a strong awareness once again of the shortage and necessity of listening to the "whys" rather than the "hows" when speaking to young adults about issues of faith, fear, and trust.

Not long after that evening, I stopped by that church and talked to the associate pastor. I told him how I was struck by his exchange with Mr. Billy. He laughed and said he and Billy had a trusting relationship that allowed them to speak truth to each other. He gave me several examples of past discussions that had brought them to a level of honesty. As I turned to leave, my friend stopped me with a question. He said, "Do you think young adults are looking for the type of trust that Billy spoke about?" Without hesitation, I said, "I think they want it more than ever, only they don't know what it looks like or how to go about obtaining it."

He shook his head and said, "We're really in trouble, aren't we?" That realization hung in the air as we parted.

GENERATIONS APART

We indeed face issues in church life today that continue to repeat themselves with little progress in hearing or seeing each other's perspective. I am almost at peace with everyone's unwillingness to change, but what continues to amaze me is the inability of us all to accept and appreciate how our theology reflects our reality. We have all grown from the seeds planted in our lives. It would be monumental if we could accept, appreciate, and affirm that regardless of our generation.

Those in our churches who grew up during the Great Depression and lived through World War II were part of a generation that understood sacrifice and endurance. They were shaped by a world that said you must provide for yourself and those you love because no one else will save you. They counted only on themselves, their families, their communities, and Jesus. Entitlement was a virtually unknown concept. The New Deal was just that: it was a new and short-term solution to address what they believed was a temporary crisis. The goal of the initiative was to help people get back on their feet and start from modest means to provide a better life for those affected by the Depression. Living through that reality bred a theology that is almost inexplicable to their grandchildren, but it is the reality of those who built the churches on the main streets and back roads of our country. What they were taught to value and the way they invested their lives have brought us to this point in time.

I recently had a conversation with a new seminary graduate from a prestigious university. She expressed her frustration that some of the older voices in theological conversations today seem to be so out of step with present-day seminarians. She said they talk almost exclusively about pulling themselves up by their bootstraps and place a disproportionate emphasis on individual responsibility in issues of the Christian faith.

She said the focus in her theological education centered on community and shared responsibility, and she thought these elders were too self-absorbed to see what she considered to be the larger picture facing the church today. I realized I hear the same conversation in reverse when I listen to the people who frustrate her. They lament that young people are missing the point. They express frustration with the young adults who feel they deserve the same portion of power and prestige as those who have been in the trenches and fought the hard fight for decades. They believe members of the younger generation have not paid their dues and are going to throw away everything older generations have worked hard to build.

The irony is that both perspectives have merit. The "greatest generation's" theology reflects a "pull yourself up by your bootstrap" reality, and the younger generation's theology reflects their group project, latchkey, "fear of strangers," and "whatever makes you happy" reality.

Today's young adults are the manifestation and fruition of the men and women who dreamed of better things for their children and grandchildren. When they came home from WWII in the late 1940s, they immediately invested in the future. They labored for their descendants to have comfortable homes, educational opportunities, and less strenuous career choices. They sacrificed to provide luxuries that were unimaginable in their youth, and they wanted their children and grandchildren to learn to live in peace. It is amazing how quickly those desires for future generations became the expectations of those who followed.

The expectations and sense of entitlement embraced by following generations have created a cultural climate that is virtually disconnected from the driving force that created these opportunities. We speak of global warming's impact on the environment as a result of our extravagant behavior, but our lukewarm theological environment is in many ways a result of our disconnection from each other. The conversation about how we got here and where we are headed lacks mutuality. The generations that make up our theological ethos are neither listening to nor hearing each other.

The stratification of our churches has for all intents and purposes removed any opportunity for conversation between various generations. From birth, children are put into groups that rarely interact with other groups. They stay together with few adults entering their lives throughout their childhoods, and then when they reach adolescence, a mentor is hired and the church views them as "the youth group." They are showcased when they come back from trips and talk about their experience. Adults cook and even serve meals to nameless students who line up and pass with little or no interaction. Unlike my experience growing up, we speak of them as our youth, not Sarah Smith, who is Bill and Jean's girl.

The same isolation and anonymity is true of adults who create minichurches within their Sunday school classes and other church gatherings. They live out their convictions without ever having to acknowledge that there has been a seismic shift concerning issues of faith. They fail to realize that even the people in the pew do not know the biblical stories that inform a shared understanding of issues. They choose to ignore that people's religious choices are many and varied. They are oblivious to the fact that the theological question is not simply "should I be a Christian?" but "should I be a Christian, a Buddhist, a Muslim, or a pagan?" The crisis facing our churches is much larger than how to grow a Sunday school that would impress rival churches. The fabric of faith is unraveling, and the task before us is to decide what to create from the remnants.

First and foremost, we must talk about things that matter in our Christian gatherings. We must create opportunities for conversation across generational experiences, for storytelling and name recognition. Community is a bankrupt concept if the exchanging of ideas, dreams, hopes, and promise is held only within one segment of the people. There is no community without communication, appreciation, and understanding. True community engages and welcomes a variety of perspectives. It brings dissenters to the table and includes them in the conversation, rather than making outcasts of them. People with whom we disagree may have the word that moves us to the next painful but necessary step of being who Christ calls us to be. It is hard to test the spirit of someone with whom we have no relationship; it is impossible to listen to the wisdom or pain of someone whose voice we have refused to hear. We must become "generationally" bilingual. We must ask both why and how we got here and why and how we can move on from here.

Addressing an issue within an institution that shares a history and an understanding of core values usually begins with questions such as "How are we going to fix this?" or "What are we going to do now?" Those questions have served our churches well over the past millennium. The shared understanding was that as believers in Jesus Christ, we needed to construct the best and biggest programs, buildings, and memberships that we could for the glory of God. We were kingdom builders, and that was unquestionably the goal of everything we did. Therefore, "what to do" and "how to get it done" was a full-time calling. It was and is a wonderful passion, but somewhere along the way we lost our story. We failed to share the basic "whys" of what brought us to this moment in a shared Christian experience. Before most young adults can get to the "hows" of a situation, they need to know "why" we are here at all. What seems obvious to the people who have built the church that brought us to this juncture is a mystery to those who want to be part of its future. I am not sure why we are so resistant to the "why" question, but it is a major stumbling block to our shared future as communities of faith.

The unspoken attitude that says, "If you don't know what's going on, you probably don't need to be here," must change if the present church truly desires to be part of the future of Christian formation. We must address our fears and honestly and compassionately be willing to speak a word of hope, knowledge, and truth to a world that desperately wants to embrace not an ideology of religion, but a relationship, a meaningful connection with the Creator and the Shaper of lives.

The time is narrowing for the two generations to influence each other, and it will be a tragedy if we continue to withhold the riches that we all bring to the table. Somewhere over the past forty years, the fabric of trust in our world and the church has ruptured. Those in control of the assets and power of the organized church have at times developed a bunker mentality. Fear of loss has sequestered us from each other, but more importantly it has cut us off from the mission of the Christian gospel.

Why should we want to change? Why should we want to reach out and possibly lose our possessions or be hurt by someone's rejection? Why do we need to seek the lost, the lonely, and the disenfranchised? The answer is at the heart of the Christian gospel. It is what we have been called to do. We must not be afraid to ask the "why" questions. We all need to remember our purpose, our story, and mostly our Christ, who will encourage, embolden, and empower us to love again.

One of the fears of the how-askers is that the why-askers will never move beyond the exploration stage, but that fear is like being positive that every stage your firstborn enters is where he or she will remain stuck for a lifetime. People move on, they grow, and they want to affect the world they inhabit. They will get to the how, and they need someone to guide them when they arrive.

Trust takes time, however. It takes patience and presence. Developing trust is not for the fainthearted. It involves risk and uncertainty. Trust building is hard work. It means speaking to some people who come to your church ten times before they respond. There is the possibility that they will reject our ideas and the things we hold sacred, but there is also the promise that we might make a connection that changes lives. When individuals believe their stories are safe within a relationship and that the desire of others is that they be whole and valued, trust germinates and has the possibility of maturing people who can eventually reach out to others with the same willingness to risk.

When young adults come into our churches, we have expectations that are possibly beyond their present capabilities. This generation of young people has been reared in a culture of fear. From birth, they have been instructed never to speak to an adult stranger, never to take food from a stranger, and never to let an adult stranger touch them. When they come to our churches, we are often offended by their lack of friendly response when we speak to them and ask personal questions, invite them to eat with us, and want to hug them during meet and greet time. It is not that they do not want to build relationships; they are simply handicapped in developing trust, and in many ways we are responsible. Be patient and unwrap the possibilities of community gently. We must let them know that we will wait for them and that we are deserving of their trust. Then we must be trustworthy.

Conversely, young adults need to be challenged by people they trust to lift their heads, learn people's names, and invest in people's lives. It might be risky, but it is a necessary step in living in community. I was stunned when a student told me ten weeks into the semester that he did not know his professor's name. When I asked him why, he had no reason; he just didn't think it was important. The cultural myopia of young adults will certainly limit their opportunities to be enriched by the wisdom and richness of multigenerational relationships. I think of my professors who encouraged me and opened doors for me, and now I have the privilege of providing transportation to Sunday worship each week for one of those mentors.

Growing from recipient of care to provider of care is a privilege of life lived out not only in our families of origin, but in the larger family of faith for untold generations. This value of kinship was modeled, was valued by people who shaped our lives, was learned by osmosis, but all of these learning experiences require people who are willing to risk the uncertainty of relationships. If we fail to see each other respectfully as people of value and worth, we live in danger of losing that connection and the opportunity to impact each other

The impact one person has by naming the value and hope in another person is one of the most underused practices in our communities of faith today. Foundations have invested millions of dollars in conversation about "call" in the lives of younger generations, and it is wonderful to bring this conversation to the forefront. However, nothing replaces the influence of a respected mentor looking into the face of a young person and saying, "I see in you gifts and worth that can be used for the ongoing mission of the kingdom of God." Furthermore, "There is a place for you in leadership at Christ's table, and I value what you bring to ministry." For a myriad of reasons, we squander opportunity after opportunity to bless those people hungry for a word of hope. All of the reasons seem based in fear, and it is time that we all move through the fear to offer hospitality and invitation.

A LISTENING PROJECT

When I worked on my doctorate of ministry, the last requirement for graduation was the infamous project. Its proposed purpose was to help the student focus on an area of concern in one's congregation that could use attention. Since my congregation was made up solely of college students, I wanted to do something related to evangelism. Evangelism was and is an emotionally charged concept that is used to delineate Christians as evangelical or not.

Leonard Sweet was the dean of my program, and he said something the first day of class that made me want to explore this issue. I needed to view this idea of evangelism from the perspective of young adults, what the church was saying and not saying, and the value that might be gained if we spent more time listening.

Dr. Sweet said, "Young postmoderns don't want to hear our story. They want us to hear their story, and we must be able and equipped to help them see how Christ has been a part of their story all along." I called my project "Listening Evangelism" and gathered a spectrum of twelve students to help me live out this idea. It took us twelve weeks, and the last stage was an interpretation of each of their personal gospels based on three questions: When did Jesus change your life? How did that affect your life? What impact has your life had on the world entrusted to us with the gospel?

We spent the last evening of the Listening Evangelism group as we spent the previous two group gatherings, with student volunteers interpreting the "personal gospels" of the other group members. On this last evening, only one student remained who needed to listen as two of her peers interpreted her gospel for the group. Like the others, her gospel was to address the three questions above.

The two who were assigned to reflect on this person's gospel had been given three weeks to pray and ponder what they would say about her written offering. They had both come to my office to talk about what they should say to her. A great deal of pain was evident in her writings, and the interpreters were concerned about how to approach her story within the group setting.

Throughout the weeks of the project meetings, the young woman's suffering had been obvious to the group. Her demeanor and body language spoke of her struggle, but we were all at a loss as to how to help her. I knew some of the sources of her pain, but there did not seem to be any way to reach through her personal hell to touch her. It was difficult to watch, but living it was obviously more painful for her. Throughout the semester, I hoped for a sign of healing in her eyes, but it was never there. Amazingly, she was able to maintain her schoolwork and her day-to-day living. Her tenacity and her will to survive were nothing less than heroic.

During most of the group's sessions, she sat in fetal position in either the corner of the sofa or an individual chair. She seemed detached and disinterested in the proceedings of the group. Often she left the room in tears. On more than one occasion, she and I talked outside the group, and I gave her permission to step out of the project, but each time she expressed a strong desire to stay. Her best friend was in the group, and she thought it was important to stay connected. However, about four weeks into the group process, she came to me and said she needed to leave the group. I told her that I hated to see her leave, but I would honor her decision.

I had mixed emotions about her leaving. She needed to stay connected to a community of faith while she dealt with whatever was so crippling to her. My ambivalence was moot when she walked into the group session the following Sunday night and came to every other meeting for the duration of the project. The group absorbed her tortured presence without comment.

As we came to the final meeting, however, there was a mixture of relief and sadness in the room that was more encompassing than this particular student's pain. They knew that night was an ending, and they were sad for the impending loss of community. However, there was one more piece of work that needed to be carried out, and we had to be faithful to the call.

As everyone settled into their places, one of the interpreters cut her eyes at me in a pleading manner. She did not want to be the first one to explain the gospel before us that evening. There was a moment of silence, and then the other interpreter jumped in and said, "Well, I want to talk about this gospel."

This particular student interpreter brought several things to our group. One was his honesty; the other was the full disclosure of his academic struggles as a student. He told the group that he had needed to retake his freshman English courses because of his poor grasp of grammar. Therefore, when the first thing that came out of his mouth as he looked at the young woman's written gospel was, "What I see in this are a lot of fragmented sentences," we were amazed. As we stared at him with our mouths agape, he pushed on. He looked purposefully at her and said, "In those fragmented sentences, I see a lot of brokenness and pain." He went on to say, "The problem with your paper is that everyone is looking at it this way." He held up the peach-colored 8 1/2-x-11-inch paper in its vertical position so that everyone could see the blank verse style of writing on the page. "What they need to do is look at it this way," he said, and he turned it horizontally. In an instant, not only did the paper shift, but our perspective did as well.

We saw a graph, an EKG of her spiritual journey. The interpreter began to point out that at the high points of the graph were words like Messiah, God's Love, music, home, His heart, and love, and in the valleys were words like rage, screaming, anger, alone, and falling apart. There was a stunned silence in the room. The young man intently looked at her, and slowly her head rose and their eyes met. Then he said, "You know what I saw throughout this whole gospel? I saw you looking for Jesus, and I want you to know that Jesus is looking for you, and do you know what? Y'all are going to find each other!"

At that moment, she leapt out of the chair and in the middle of the circle they embraced. With a tearful hug, she said, "Thank you, Charlie. I needed to hear that."

Don't we all? Charlie listened to the story of this young woman, he unflinchingly shared her pain, he modeled honesty, and he offered her Hope with a capital "H." This is the calling of us all—young or old; introvert or extrovert; old church or new church; modern or postmodern. We are called to hear and respond to those who surround us, and it is a mighty calling.

Chapter 6

21ST-CENTURY ANCIENT PRACTICES

Cathy Payne Anderson

INTO ANCIENT PRAYER PRACTICES

I grew up as the daughter of a Baptist preacher who was the son of a Baptist preacher who was the son of another Baptist preacher in south Mississippi. To say that "being Baptist" is in my blood is something of an understatement. In describing my faith tradition, I often use the phrase "Deep South Baptist"—this phrase evokes for me images of small country churches, dinners on the ground, revivals, Vacation Bible School, and Bible drills. These places and practices form the backdrop for all I know about myself and all I know about God. The saints in those hard, straight-backed wooden pews loved me, explained Scripture to me, prayed for me, and cheered me on as I traveled toward adulthood and professional ministry.

In the care of these believers, I learned that God loves me and listens to my prayers. They taught me that prayer is conversation with the Creator of the Universe. They believed in "praying from the heart" and were suspicious of any ritualized prayers. (The one exception to this was Jesus' "model prayer," which they call "The Lord's Prayer." I suppose that since Jesus said to pray it, it was okay.) In most times of prayer, I was expected to sit (or stand) quietly, bow my head, and close my eyes. While I don't remember anyone telling me that God should be addressed as "Thou," I certainly learned by listening to the way the adults in my life addressed God. The "Deep South Baptists" of my childhood avoided anything that smacked of liturgy. We didn't even use the word (although we certainly had one). We didn't have "litanies" in our bulletin; we had "responsive readings" in our hymnals.

I can imagine the surprise on the faces of these dear friends if they were to hear me talking today about ancient Christian practices that have become central to my faith life. They would never dream of walking a labyrinth or praying a "breath prayer." The practices of examen and lectio divina would be as foreign to their Baptist hearts as the sounds of the Latin names would be to their Baptist ears. And yet, these four practices have become vital pathways of communication between God and me.

I arrived in this strange land of ancient faith gradually, step by step. One image I have for my journey is of a child collecting pieces of a jigsaw puzzle for which she has no box and, therefore, no idea of the complete picture. In isolated moments of my life, God would give me a solitary piece, or a handful of pieces, and I would stick them in my pocket. Occasionally I pulled them out, mulled them over, maybe even found one or two that fit together, but never could I see the picture. I learned to find joy in the individual pieces, to see the beauty in their colors and shapes. I began to watch for them and clap my hands in glee when one surprised me along the way.

I can remember my youth group in Texas pretending to be first-century Christians and living in fear for our lives. This was probably my first experience with separating faith from my personal context. This was the first time I understood that being a follower of Jesus and being a Deep South Baptist were not the same thing. (One piece goes into the pocket.) My understanding was broadened during the years that I worked with the Columbia Drive Baptist Church in Decatur, Georgia. I ministered with youth and children from two congregations made up of immigrants from the country of Laos, both Hmong and Lao people. As I learned the rhythms of their worship and grew to love and respect the practices of their faith heritage, I was opened more than ever to traditions beyond my own. (There goes another puzzle piece.)

Immediately following my two years at Columbia Drive, I moved to Louisville, Kentucky, to begin my seminary training. It was there that I met ancient mystics (long dead but available to me in their writings) who would become my traveling companions for the next two decades (so far). I took a class titled "Classics of Christian Devotion." I soaked in the writings of Julian of Norwich, Thomas Merton, St. Augustine, Brother Lawrence, Søren Kierkegaard, Thomas Kelly, and Pierre Teilhard de Chardin. I found in these believers kindred spirits—people for whom life with God was not nearly so "cut and dry" as I had grown up believing it to be. Each of these friends loved God with a passion that I had not heard expressed in my limited context. I wanted to know them, to be companions, to learn from them their passion for the God we both loved. As I read their writings and pondered their paths, puzzle pieces rained down all around me.

The writings of Brother Lawrence in particular resonated with me. I have an innate tendency to be in constant conversation with God. I can remember walking the halls of my high school, smiling as I shared a secret joke with God. God was the One to whom I turned when I needed to laugh or cry or scream. Brother Lawrence seemed to share this type of intimate, day-to-day friendship with God.

The first time I read *The Practice of the Presence of God*, I underlined entire pages and continually muttered to myself "yes, that's it—yes!" Brother Lawrence literally "practiced" being in God's presence every minute of every day. He considered every act of his daily living as an expression of his love for God. He washed dishes for God and mended shoes for God. Brother Lawrence eventually gave up his order's regular required prayers in favor of practicing constant prayer. He wrote, "I make it my priority to persevere in His holy presence, wherein I maintain a simple attention and a fond regard for God, which I may call an actual presence of God."[1] He spoke in intimate terms about the God of the universe. This way of seeing God was very familiar to me and my Deep-South Baptist understanding of having a "personal relationship with Jesus." Perhaps the most important thing I learned from Brother Lawrence is not to waste any time regretting moments spent out of God's presence. Instead, we should just walk back into God's presence. Guilt is not what God wants from me—adoration is.

In sharp contrast to the peaceful, loving relationship described by Brother Lawrence was the gut-wrenching, painful, ecstatic relationship with God described by Julian of Norwich. Her writings, so full of graphic depictions of both the suffering of Jesus and her own suffering, were completely foreign to me. They served to open my mind and heart to a more difficult side of life with God. Sometimes life is horrible and painful. Instead of running from this pain, Julian leaned into it and found God there. I learned from Julian to trust that God is in every moment, even the horrible ones.

These companions (and many others I met on the way) walked with me through my seminary years, early years of ministry, and family life. I went through a particularly dark season that included the sickness and death of my beloved preacher father and my own clinical depression. I had struggled with depression off and on for most of my life since adolescence but was not diagnosed or treated until I was thirty-three. During these darkest of times, my old mystic friends became increasingly important. I also met new friends who would take my faith life in a direction I could not have imagined. I found the "new Christians."

I first read Brian McLaren's *A New Kind of Christian* in 2002, smack in the middle of my "dark season." Reading the struggles of a burned-out pastor, Dan, and the subsequent conversations he had with Neo echoed the pain and darkness of my own life during that time. I longed to have someone who could walk with me and remind me of God's presence in the midst of my suffering the way Neo walked with Pastor Dan. I found that this book provided an opening to conversation with other believers who struggled with some of the same issues. Conversations became friendships. Friendships became pathways of communication between me and this God whom I was desperate to love, but who seemed so distant in my darkness. I was open to whatever path lay before me as long as it ended in a passionate, loving relationship with God

In the years that followed, these "new Christians" became not only companions but prophets. They spoke light into the dark places of my faith that had become bogged down in institutional church life. The life of a church staff minister, or as I often call it, being a "professional Christian," seemed to be a life that chose me instead of a life I chose. I was waiting on my "call to ministry" for as long as I could remember. Making a commitment to that call at the age of fourteen seemed like a natural next step in my walk with God. Ministry was, literally, my family business. I knew the ropes, went to the right school, worked the system, and knew the people I needed to know to be successful in my chosen field. I quickly discovered, however, that the business side of ministry had the potential to drain every ounce of life out of my being. While I loved pastoral care and music and preaching and teaching and simply being with church members, I loathed budgets and batteries and volunteer schedules and business meetings and attendance goals and performance evaluations. Church, which had always been home to me, gradually became a place I dreaded going. Years later, I heard Barbara Brown Taylor say this of her decision to leave local church ministry: "My role and my soul were eating each other alive." I so understood how she felt.

Then the prophets began to speak to me. I began to hear about a different way to be in faith community, a way that had little to do with a building at an address and all the needs housed therein. Instead, this way was more about finding friends with whom I could live my faith intentionally. This way involved understanding my place in the larger family of God-followers and understanding how my life affects everyone else's lives. I read a book called *Sabbath Sense* by Donna Schaper. Rev. Schaper, much like the ancient mystics of my seminary days, called me to a vision of everyday faith that was simultaneously totally foreign and completely familiar. She spoke of Sabbath as being less of a day with certain practices and expectations, and more of a way of relating to time and space and God. She wrenched the concept of Jubilee out of the Old Testament's hold and thrust it into my life. She empowered me to take small steps in my own life toward Jubilee "like being less perfectionistic. . . . Like breaking our enslavement to our clocks and calendars. . . . Like believing in a deeper sense of time, and river, and rock."[2]

I began to share this book with anyone who would listen to me. I became intentional about *being* rather than *doing*. I celebrated the Sabbath sense that already existed in my life and cultivated new spaces for Sabbath in my daily routine. I became passionate about practicing the presence of God in these new spaces.

Puzzle pieces piled up in my pockets. Four key pieces, however, were yet to come: lectio divina, examen, breath prayer, and labyrinth walking. In the pages that follow, we will look at each of these practices, both its history and its story in my journey with God.

LECTIO DIVINA

I first encountered lectio divina, or holy reading, at a CBF Young Leaders retreat in 2000. During the worship service one night, the leader called us to prayer, using this ancient practice. The practice itself is quite simple. Scripture is read repeatedly, aloud if possible, and then meditated upon as to what God is saying *to me today*.

Devotional reading of Scripture has been around for millennia. The psalmist writes of devotional Scripture reading in Psalm 1:1-3:

> Blessed are those
> who do not walk in step with the wicked
> or stand in the way that sinners take
> or sit in the company of mockers,
> but who delight in the law of the Lord
> and meditate on his law day and night.
> They are like a tree planted by streams of water,
> which yields its fruit in season
> and whose leaf does not wither—
> whatever they do prospers (TNIV)

While my first experience was in a corporate worship setting, lectio has traditionally been practiced in solitude. The practice we know as lectio divina was formalized by the Benedictine monks in the way they lived out the Rule of St. Benedict during the dark ages. In particular, a Benedictine monk named Guigo II laid out a basic pattern still followed today: reading, meditation, prayer, and contemplation.[3] According to the web site www.lectio-divina.org, "Lectio Divina is ordinarily confined to the slow perusal of sacred Scripture, both the Old and New Testaments; it is undertaken not with the intention of gaining information but of using the texts as an aide to contact the living God."[4]

Group practice is a more recent modification of the ancient practice. The night I first experienced lectio, a passage of Scripture was read aloud two times (by two different voices). The worship leader instructed us to listen for the word or phrase that jumped out at us. We were to ponder that word or phrase as we listened. The passage was read again (by a third voice), and this time we listened for how that word or phrase connected to our lives at that moment. Where was Christ reaching out to us in this word or phrase? The final reading was for us to discern what Christ was calling us to do through this text. Because this experience was inside a worship service, there was not much sharing aloud. In a smaller group setting (ideally four to eight), each person would have the opportunity to share reflections on the questions asked for each reading. I have found the practice of lectio divina to be a powerful way to build community in small groups. I have also found new meaning and comfort in ancient Scriptures as I practice solitary lectio divina.

BREATH PRAYER

A second practice that has become meaningful to me is "breath prayer." Breath prayer is a form of contemplative prayer, specifically a form of centering prayer. I encountered this way of praying during my first experience with leading a Companions in Christ small group.[5] Contemplative prayer involves opening oneself up to God with no agenda other than spending time in God's presence. My way of understanding this is that it is less about my talking to God and more about my listening for God, waiting to hear what God will say and go where God's presence will take me.

A breath prayer is simply a short (seven or eight syllables) phrase that can be prayed in one breath (and with every breath). Many Christians through history and around the world have used this form of prayer in response to the biblical mandate to "pray without ceasing" (1 Thess 5:17). One familiar breath prayer is the Jesus Prayer: "Lord Jesus Christ, have mercy on me, a sinner" from Luke 18:13. This is sometimes shortened to "Lord Jesus, have mercy. " I often choose portions of Scripture I am studying or memorizing. It could be a phrase that has grabbed my attention during a lectio divina. I regularly pray the first line from Psalm 103: "Bless the Lord, O my soul." Breath prayers do not necessarily have to come from Scripture. A line in the song "River God" by Nichole Nordeman says, "when the sunset comes my prayer will be this one, that you might pick me up and notice that I am just a little smoother in your hand."[6] From that lyric I have lifted the phrase "just a little smoother" as a way of opening myself up to God's transforming of me in this present moment.

EXAMEN

The third practice, examen, is the one to which I have most recently been introduced. Rick Bennett (my contemplative spirituality hero) introduced the practice of examen at a gathering of Baptist Christian educators in the spring of 2008. Rick began by telling a story from the book *Sleeping with Bread: Holding What Gives You Life*, which is an excellent primer on the practice of examen. The title comes from the story of World War II orphans who had been left to starve. Once they were rescued and taken to refugee camps, many had trouble sleeping. They were afraid that they would wake up homeless and hungry again. Finally someone came up with the idea of giving each child a piece of bread to sleep with. "All through the night the bread reminded them, 'today I ate and I will eat again tomorrow.'"[7]

Ignatius of Loyola created his "spiritual exercises," which describe examen as instructions for spiritual direction. The practice was for spiritual directors to lead participants through a five-week retreat spent examining their lives and God's work in their lives. My version of the practice of examen is much simpler and comes from the Linns' book. Each night I ask myself, "What gave me life today and what drained my life today?" The practice allows me to see God at work in my day. By naming the parts of my day that gave me life, I name the parts where I was aware of God's moving in my life. When I name the parts of my day that drained me, I name the parts where something (myself or something outside myself) stemmed the tide of God's moving in my life. If there are sins that need forgiveness (and there usually are), I can name them, repent, and put them to rest. By the way, this part of the practice would feel familiar to my Deep-South Baptist friends—

confessing our sins and trusting that God will remove them "as far as the east is from the west."[8] Then, as I go to sleep, I "hold on to" the part of my day that brought me life. Rick tells of a modification of this practice that he does with his children at bedtime. Each night he asks each child, "Where did you see God today?"

I find that examen opens me to peace and rest that God offers me each night. I am often reminded of Psalm 42:8, which says, "By day the LORD directs his love, at night his song is with me—a prayer to the God of my life" (NIV). There have been seasons in my life when sleep was impossible, times of deep despair or overwhelming stress. Some of them have lasted weeks, even months. None of them, however, have come since I learned to practice examen. Even though there have been serious stressors in my life since then, I am always able to sleep. I believe there is something to this idea of "holding what gives you life."

LABYRINTHS

Of all the ancient practices, the one that is the closest to my heart and most influential in my life is also the one that would seem strangest to those dear Deep-South Baptist saints who raised me—labyrinth walking. I don't remember my first experience with a labyrinth. I do remember the one that opened my life to the power of the practice. One day in fall 2006 I walked out of a particularly disturbing church staff meeting in which we had discussed heartbreaking issues like child abuse, infuriating issues like power struggles, and mundane frustrations like budget cuts. I was completely exhausted physically, emotionally, and spiritually. I grabbed my Bible and my journal, jumped in my car, and drove away, not sure where I was headed. Earlier in the week, I had read about an outdoor labyrinth at the Cathedral of St. Phillip in Atlanta. I drove the fifteen minutes from my church to that church, concentrating on breathing in and breathing out. A song by Steven Curtis Chapman played in my head that included the line, "these are the days when the blind lead the blind."[9] That was exactly how I felt about life in my line of work. I had no idea what God was going to say to me, but I certainly had some questions for God and I intended to ask them.

I found the church, found the entrance to the parking lot (on the third try), parked, and sat in my car trying to figure out what I was doing there. Eventually I gathered my Bible, journal, pen, and courage and walked to the entrance of the labyrinth. It is a beautifully landscaped labyrinth modeled after the one in the floor of the cathedral in Chartres, France. I laid my things on a bench, said a quick prayer, and began walking. Because the path is narrow (and my feet are not), I had to take care with each step. The path winds in and out, back and forth, slowly making its way to the center. As I walked, I began to experience some sort of peace—perhaps from the rhythm of my footsteps or the steadiness of my breathing or the singing of the birds around me. I wound around and around, never sure where the next turn would take me, trusting that the path would eventually lead to the center, the part of the labyrinth that represents the presence of God. Once I had walked all the way in and all the way out, I sat and pondered the experience. My journal from that day records the following reflections:

> So many times so near the center, but never all the way
> Stretches seem straight, but there was always a bend ahead
> Going out the way I came in, the path was familiar but everything was backwards

There it was. The amazing parallel between the walking experience and my life with God. There are many times when I feel like I am walking directly toward God when, in fact, I am walking away from God. Many days the path seems to be straight and easy, and then, before I know it, a bend catches me off guard. Sometimes the life of faith is simply disorienting, and I feel a little dizzy. I spent the rest of that afternoon sitting on a bench, reading random Scriptures, writing out all my angry questions, and waiting for God to respond. And somehow, by some miracle, God did respond. By the time I got back to work that afternoon, my whole attitude had been redeemed. I believed again that God was directing my path and I could relax, follow, and see where we would go.

In the weeks, months, and years since that fall day, labyrinth walking has become for me a sacred Sabbath practice. I try to spend one day a month at a labyrinth, listening. During these days, God speaks directly to my heart in ways that I cannot hear in other places or through other practices. A poem by Jill Kimberly Hartwell Geoffrion expresses the welcome I feel at a labyrinth:

WELCOME TO THE LABYRINTH
You're here!
This is the well
You have been seeking.

Put down your luggage anywhere;
It will be attended to.

That distinctive scent is from a burning candle.
Love lit it—in anticipation of your arrival.

Beauty will help you get oriented.
She usually suggests,
"Leave your shoes by the front door."

Please make yourself at home.[10]

I often memorize Scripture and do a form of lectio divina while walking the labyrinth. I believe there is something about the rhythm of walking that opens me to God. I've also introduced labyrinth walking to my family. My husband and daughters have walked labyrinths with me all across the southeastern United States. We make an effort to find a labyrinth any time we visit a new city. I've begun collecting pictures of these labyrinths as a sort of spiritual travel log. My oldest daughter, Gracie, was eight the first time I took her with me to walk a labyrinth. At the entrance to this particular labyrinth, the church had placed a mailbox with strips of paper containing Scriptures and prayers. Gracie pulled out a prayer, took it with her, and said it over and over as she walked the labyrinth. As we drove, she said, "Mom, do you want to hear my prayer? I memorized it!" I was overwhelmed by her desire to connect to God in a way I hadn't imagined she could experience, much less express.

One of my favorite aspects of labyrinth walking is this: there is no way to get lost. There are no wrong turns or false paths. You will always arrive at the center, as long as you keep walking. Somewhere along the way I heard a saying: "The only way to get unstuck is to just start moving." Labyrinth walking has become for me a favorite way to get "unstuck" in my journey of faith.

I do wonder sometimes what Miss Alice, my third grade Training Union teacher, would say if I brought her with me to a labyrinth and talked about lectio or contemplative prayer or examen. I wonder if I will ever be able to explain the puzzle pieces I've been collecting all these years to those wonderful Baptist saints of my youth. I wonder if I'll ever know what the picture on the top of the box really looks like. As my pockets fill, the image is just beginning to take shape. It has something to do with a way of being church that is life-giving rather than life-draining. There is beauty and richness and depth that I cannot yet see, but I am confident they are there. I'm just keeping my eyes open, walking around the next bend, hoping I don't miss a single piece of the wonderful life God has for me, and thanking God for the amazing companions I've joined along the way.

Notes

1. Brother Lawrence, *The Practice of The Presence of God*, Light Heart Edition, www.practicegodspresence.com.

2. Donna Schaper, *Sabbath Sense: A Spiritual Antidote for the Overworked* (Philadelphia: Innisfree Press, Inc. 1997) 120.

3. Tony Jones, *The Sacred Way* (Grand Rapids: Zondervan Publishing, 2005) 50. I have found Tony Jones's book to be an excellent resource in introducing these practices to people who have never encountered them.

4. http://www.lectio-divina.org/index.cfm.

5. Companions in Christ is a small group curriculum based on spiritual practices. Information is available at www.companionsinchrist.org.

6. Nichole Nordeman, "River God," on *Wide Eyed*, CD, Star Song Music, 1998.

7. Dennis Linn, Shelia Fabricant Linn, Matthew Linn, *Sleeping with Bread: Holding What Gives You Life* (New York: Paulist Press, 1995).

8. Psalm 103:12.

9. Steven Curtis Chapman, "Blind Lead the Blind," on *For the Sake of the Call*, CD, Sparrow, 1990.

10. Jill Kimberly Hartwell Geoffrion, *Christian Prayer and Labyrinths: Pathways to Faith, Hope, and Love* (Cleveland OH: Pilgrim Press, 2004) 21.

Chapter 7

MAKING SPACE AT THE TABLE

Christina Whitehouse-Suggs

MAKING SOME ROOM

"Don't go. Stay. We'll take a collection and you can be *our* pastor."

The words alone were enough to make me weep. Honest, authentic, transparent love for who I was and what I had meant, validation for all I'd done.

How much more, then, did it mean that those words came from a deaf Muslim man? How to respond to the nods of agreement from interpreters and other deaf friends around the table, none of whom were Christians?

Maybe I should start with how I ended up in that moment.

Growing up as a Baptist preacher's kid in Miami, Florida, might have had something to do with it. I was definitely in the minority anywhere I went. (Baptists in Miami?) Believe it or not, there were a few of us. Only . . . it always seemed like I was a little different from the other Baptists I met. Maybe it was because the church where I grew up was a diverse little band of folks from all walks of life. My youth group was made up of African Americans, Cubans, Haitians, and Koreans, and I was one of the only semi-Anglos (my mom is Puerto Rican). Maybe it was because we had three to four worship services happening simultaneously throughout the building in different languages. Maybe it was simply that my family taught me that love and a huge meal around our table (where anyone was welcome) was how the kingdom of God might look.

Maybe it had to do with attending public school where I became friends with a loud Jewish kid who invited me to his Bar Mitzvah—the beginning of a deep friendship that continues today. Maybe it was the kindness my Buddhist friend showed me when I visited her home and asked incessant questions about their statues and altars throughout the house. Or maybe it was when my Wiccan friend told me that my "aura was so warm and welcoming—not like those other Christians."

Most of the time I felt like I was constantly trying to balance the messages I got at church—"Without Jesus, you are lost!"—with my love for friends who accepted me, quirks and all. How do I balance the message that God loves everyone with the idea that there were conditions placed on that love? What was I to do with my friends who struggled with their sexuality? What was I to say to my friend from youth group who came to me in tears, confessing that he didn't want to be "an abomination" but was tired of fighting, that he still loved God and believed in Jesus despite his sexual orientation?

I confess that I struggled for many years with these dual messages. "Repent and be saved!" versus "God is love, and those who abide in love abide in God, and God abides in them." I wish I'd known Chuck Poole back then. I wish someone like him had told me, "Let's just admit it; we're all just picking and choosing our way through the Bible. Picking and choosing the verses that fit our worldview and confirm our prejudices and stereotypes; ignoring the ones that make us uncomfortable or challenge us."[1]

You're probably thinking, "So when did it happen? When did the shift occur?" When did I finally embrace the radical notion of hospitality as being not only a spiritual gift God had given me but also my responsibility as a follower of Christ? Obviously, the seeds were planted in a variety of ways, but what made them take root and grow?

I can point to a few touchstones along my journey of faith where my "radical hospitality" has gotten me into trouble with my more conservative friends as well as endeared me to those who have been disenfranchised by the church for a long time. I can also offer shameful moments when I "toed the party line" instead of speaking of the truth and grace I had experienced firsthand. Other than that, there wasn't a Damascus road kind of experience about it. It was a series of small steps that only make sense when viewed in hindsight.

Let me offer you the snapshots first. You've already seen a few from my childhood/adolescent years in Miami. Here's another one: It's the late 1980s and I'm a teenager. Sebastian,[2] a homosexual man in his thirties, begins attending worship at my home church. Nothing about him (or Herman, his partner) draws our attention or makes us wonder about his sexuality. We only discovered that later, when he approached my dad about starting an AIDS ministry to people in the surrounding area of the church, including the port of Miami and cruise employees. He wanted to do this because he and Herman were both infected and thought that if our little community of faith could love them, we might be able to love other disenfranchised folks.

If you'll indulge me for a moment, allow me to digress. Since I was part of the "MTV Generation," that meant being aware of AIDS in a different way. It meant that I heard about Ryan White and the discrimination he faced and watched Becca and Jesse deal with a teenage relationship affected by HIV in the television series *Life Goes On*. At the same time, the AIDS epidemic was still largely referred to as a "gay disease." People still thought you could contract it via mosquito bite or casual contact (i.e., hugging), and few (if any) churches were involved with providing ministry of *any* kind. The virus wasn't understood or well controlled, and medication was more about managing pain at the end of life than keeping the disease in check. So "AIDS ministry" was more like hospice or palliative care than anything else.

Despite all of these things, I watched my dad learn about HIV and AIDS so that he could educate our congregation and help them embrace this new ministry. He led by example: hugging Sebastian and Herman, taking them to doctor's appointments, researching treatment options, and eventually performing Herman's funeral. I don't remember anyone making a big deal over their sexuality; the only thing that mattered was that they were members of our church, they were sick and dying, and we loved them.

Years later, I asked my dad why he chose to do something so risky. What prompted him to choose grace when every other Baptist I knew spoke words of condemnation? His answer: "It was the right thing to do. It's what Jesus did; binding up the wounds of the brokenhearted and welcoming the outcast."

If you knew my dad, you'd know that he's not a "rock-the-boat" kind of guy. He doesn't do things deliberately to push people's buttons or make them uncomfortable. But his example of radical hospitality is firmly planted in my heart and mind and reminds me that sometimes the answer is as simple as "It's the right thing to do."

Here's another snapshot: It's the late 1990s and I'm in my undergraduate studies at a Baptist university in North Carolina. I serve as a leader in the Baptist Student Union and am active in the Student Government Association, doing well in classes I enjoy, and working part-time as a youth minister at a local church. My roommate, Tori, is a new Christian who struggles with the social implications of her faith decision.

Let me unpack that a bit. Tori is on the soccer team, which has a reputation for being wild and antagonistic toward Christians. She comes back from practice one day and drops the bomb: "So, you wanna be the chaplain for the women's soccer team?"

What?

Apparently, some of the women have been in classes with me, think I am "pretty cool," and would like me to be their chaplain. Again, let me explain what that means: by having me as their chaplain, the hard-core evangelicals who are out to "save their souls" will finally leave them alone.

My first meeting with the team occurs at a party where I'm handed a beer with everyone watching to see how I'll respond. I take a big swig, look around the room, and say, "Hi, my name is Christina and I'm a Baptist who drinks." The room explodes with laughter and I know I've passed the first test.

I pass the second test by keeping my prayer in the locker room short and sweet and focusing on keeping everyone safe on the field. I pass the third test with flying colors by almost getting thrown out of a game for heckling the referee after a bad call.

The fourth test is more difficult to negotiate. I go out to eat with some of the team members after a particularly bad loss, and I know they just want to drink it away. Somehow the conversation takes an unexpected turn when Maggie and Sarah reveal to me that they are dating and wait for my response. I haven't quite worked out how I feel about homosexuality or exactly what I believe, but I choose to smile and ask how long they've been together. They tell me, I relate some story about my boyfriend, and the conversation moves on. We spend the rest of the evening laughing, eating, and having a good time. Apparently since I didn't freak out and condemn them to hell, all is well.

After I drop everyone off at their dorms except Maggie and am parking the car (just when I think I'm in the clear), she asks me what I think about her being gay. "What do you believe?" she asks, looking anxiously into my eyes for some grace as I fumble with my keys.

Here comes my moment of shame.

I wish I'd said something like, "I don't really know. I know what I've been told and what I think I understand from reading the Bible, but I just don't know. I think God loves everyone, and that's how I'm trying to live my life, too."

Instead, I stammer, "Well, the Bible says it's a sin. But we're all sinners and there's no distinction between my sin and yours. God loves us all despite our sin. And the Bible also says we shouldn't judge others so I try to remember that. I mean, I don't agree with your lifestyle but I still want to be your friend."

It's cold as we walk back to our dorm. Maggie has her hands in her jacket and her head down against the wind. I'm shivering, either from cold or nerves, and my gut clenches, waiting to see her reaction. She is silent as we cross the street and I see tears in her eyes. I want to say something, to take it all back, anything! But I don't. When we reach the pathway to my dorm, she just nods at me and keeps walking.

I stand there for a moment, watching her walk away, and I know I've failed her. I have slammed the door of grace and forgiveness on her, and she is the outcast once again. I realize that I am no better than the hard-core evangelicals trying to save her soul and, in fact, have probably done more damage than they were capable of doing.

One last snapshot: It's the early 2000s and I'm a full-time, self-employed sign language interpreter *and* a full-time seminary student (not something I'd recommend, by the way).

My husband and I have been recommended by the dean for two part-time staff positions at a large church in North Carolina. We are humbled by his faith in us and shocked at how quickly the process leads to a call. This means selling our house and cars, leaving the church where we were affirmed in our call to ministry, moving to a different town, and quitting our jobs.

You're probably thinking, "What's the big deal?"

Working in the deaf community is complicated. You can't just learn the language in class or from a book; it requires socializing with the same clients for whom you have interpreted private meetings and doctor appointments. You must be able to maintain confidentiality at all costs and remain neutral in the midst of an assignment. No interjecting options or allowing your worldview to shade your interpretation. Once you're accepted as someone who genuinely cares about the deaf community, that you aren't just in it for the money, it's almost impossible to leave the field because people have invested so much of themselves in you. Which leads me back to the scene that opens this chapter:

"Don't go. Stay. We'll take a collection and you can be *our* pastor."

The words alone were enough to make me weep. Honest, authentic, transparent love for who I was and what I had meant, validation for all I'd done.

How much more, then, did it mean that those words came from a deaf Muslim man? How to respond to the nods of agreement from interpreters and other deaf friends around the table, none of whom were Christians?

It was our going-away party, and they were making it hard to leave. These wonderful, diverse people with whom I'd shared meals, interpreted weddings and ultrasounds, and discussed spiritual matters wanted me to know that I was not only a colleague but a friend. Despite the differences in our backgrounds and beliefs, they knew they could trust me with their pain and their joy.

I realized I was on holy ground in that moment. All I could do was weep.

These are some of the experiences that informed my theological education and converged to create my current understanding of hospitality. Life-changing? Yes. Dramatic? Not in my option, no. Certainly there was no one event that tipped me over the edge or caused me to radically alter how I interacted with people. Attending a seminary that encouraged me to think for myself and form my own theology as opposed to indoctrinating me was probably what gave me permission to finally embrace the idea of hospitality as being central to how I live out my faith. Additionally, I was given the language I needed to articulate just how important it is to accept those who are different.

Theologian Miroslav Volf's book, *Exclusion and Embrace: A Theological Exploration of Identity, Otherness, and Reconciliation,* finally helped me understand the idea of embracing "the other" (or one part of hospitality) as an essential element of a theology of reconciliation. While reading this book, I had one of those "A-ha!" moments. My love for others who are different from me, my insatiable curiosity about their lives and cultures all made sense within the framework of reconciliation. God is continually at work reconciling all of creation. If I understand that the Holy Spirit lives and breathes and moves within me, doesn't it make sense that I would possess the same desire for reconciliation?

It's probably telling that the first sermon I ever wrote was titled "Reclaiming Hospitality." The Scripture was John 6:1-13, the feeding of the multitude, the only story to occur in all four Gospels. In John's account, there is no breaking of bread or prayer to accompany the miracle—just a brief word of thanks before Jesus distributes the food himself. There is the sense of Jesus as gracious host, giving not because he is required to do so but out of grace and generosity. Imagine the scene: everyone eating together, unified by a common meal served by a loving host.

Christine Pohl's book, *Making Room: Recovering Hospitality as a Christian Tradition*, was also significant in helping me articulate my theology. She claims that the New Testament shows Jesus as simultaneously guest, host, and meal. He is guest whenever we welcome and care for the stranger and the broken. He is host when he provides for those who don't ask or expect to be fed. He is our meal as we feed on his life to nourish ours.

That is how I try to live: with a humble understanding that I have been the recipient of extravagant grace, that I have been nourished by spiritual bread in order to care for others. It is my joy and responsibility as a follower of Christ to provide for those who don't ask or expect to be fed. To point toward the God who is reconciling you and me and all of creation.

I'm just trying to make some space at the table.

Notes

1. Quote by Chuck Poole during the theme interpretation at the Cooperative Baptist Fellowship General Assembly, Memphis TN, 2008.

2. All names have been changed to protect privacy.

Chapter 8

AMOS'S RAIN DANCE

Greg Jarrell

EAST ST. LOUIS

The only thing I knew about East St. Louis was that pretty much everyone told me I did not want to be there, so I applied and was accepted for a summer mission position at the Baptist-run Christian Activity Center in the city through my college's Baptist Student Union. I embarked following my sophomore year at school in small-town, very white Boone, North Carolina. At this point in my journey, I was still unencumbered by ideas like "social justice" or "preferential option for the poor." I was just a young guy who loved Jesus, who was dealing with a call to ministry, and who felt a persistent tug to spend a few summer months on mission bringing help to some unfortunate souls.

I recall my first day in East St. Louis clearly. The center director Chet picked me up at the airport and took me on a driving tour of town. From the first moment there, I was petrified. It seemed God had played some kind of joke on me, planting me in an outpost of the third world. I had only signed up for ten weeks in St. Louis. When we stopped in the middle of a street covered in litter and lined with vacant lots to talk to a young man Chet knew, my fear increased exponentially. The only thing that kept me from locking my car door at that moment was that I knew such a gesture would alert Chet that I was terrified. The fear of being found out only slightly topped my fear for my life. So I decided to be brave, but alert—constantly checking our back and our flanks to make sure no gang of angry black youth was beginning to surround us. Chet chatted away like everything was fine. Thank goodness *one* of us was not so nonchalant in this situation. We needed to exercise caution here, not stop amid a swath of abandoned blocks and such obvious danger. The conversation finally ended and we drove away, Chet grinning and talking and me exhausted already. I wondered for a minute whether those voices of warning were right.

We arrived unharmed a few minutes later at my summer home, a room above the center overlooking the projects. I got the news that I would stay there alone for the first week. Looking out my window into the huge housing project next door, I knew I could not stay there—not by myself, at least. My imagination ran wild concerning the awful possibilities that might befall me. I must confess that I chickened out, leaving each night to crash in a variety of whiter places—a college dorm room, on a couch, and in a motel room until the permanent resident of the building returned. I was not proud of this. I even sensed within myself that this was not the right or even the sensible thing to do. But my system was shocked beyond what I could bear. Where am I? Who am I? How did I wind up here? The questions were too many and the place too overwhelming to get any perspective. I no longer knew myself, I lacked the perspective to understand my surroundings, and I had not yet acquired the wisdom to listen to my fears or to the voices that would teach me to settle them.

I did not know it at the time, but from day one, even from hour one, I was confronted with my racism. Perhaps unwittingly, the folks walking down the street or playing dice outside my window at night were prophets telling me the truth about myself. At first, the truth was too difficult to bear. I told myself that my fear of staying in East St. Louis those first nights was about being in a place that was dangerous and might jeopardize my personal safety. I know now that my fear was not external to myself. It was masked well as something else, but at root my fear was of being alone with my irrational fear—of being alone with myself. My fear was about being confronted with the truth about myself that I could not yet stand to see. I was racist, albeit subtly, and now the tables were turned. I was the minority. I lacked the power that I had in nearly every situation of my Caucasian world. I was no longer in control. I might have remained that way, except for the grace meted out by the prophet Alcurtis.

Curt, as we called him, was the embodiment of my fears. He was huge, with massive biceps and a chiseled torso. He had tattoos and wore a rag on his head. And he was angry. If there is anything that white boys like me fear, it is angry black men. Curt did not fool around. He went about his business, which largely consisted of intimidating the hell out of whoever dared to question his skills or his foul calls on the basketball court. Curt never backed down from a conflict. On the street or in the gym, it was clear that no one messed with Curt.

But for whatever reason, Curt began to pay attention to me. Our daily competition on the basketball court quickly opened me up to him, and him up to me. We began to talk some in the center or around the neighborhood. After a day or two, he did not scare me so much anymore. I learned from my coworkers that Curt had sickly parents who needed lots of care and that he was helping to raise a mentally handicapped brother ten years younger than himself. I learned that at least part of Curt's anger was due to his best friend's brutal murder only two years earlier. I saw him laugh and smile occasionally, even around me. Just one year apart in age, Curt and I were becoming friends. We came from worlds apart—further apart than I had imagined was possible in America. But there we stood, an odd pair learning to care for one another. Our friendship grew in a few short days. The prophet Curt had begun my training in the way of deeper discipleship.

Curt was not alone, of course. Hundreds of children and youth and a handful of adults began to be my teachers, and I quickly became a willing, though often dense, learner. After living in fear for a week, I began to walk around the neighborhood, to escort kids to their homes, to sit on the neighbor's front porch and listen to the Cardinals' game on the radio in the evenings. The folks all around drew me into their life together by their kindness, even in the context of one of the most violent neighborhoods in the country. In short, I quickly took the leap from missionary-helper to neighbor. It was the most important step toward conversion I had yet taken.

My ten weeks in East St. Louis confirmed my sense of call to ministry and gave it direction. I still had lots of questions. Chief among them was the question of why a place like East St. Louis even exists. Why should so many children suffer? Why do my new friends and neighbors endure cycles of poverty while I live in relative ease? Why should this injustice continue to exist in a world of God's abundance? What is God calling me to do about it? I was headed to a Baptist seminary in preparation for ministry and to seek answers to my questions. I wound up finding answers in two different places: from a group of close friends who dared to ask questions with me about injustice and about God's call on our lives, and from my neighbors.

By either providence or serendipity, I wound up living in an old working-class neighborhood called Oregon Hill. The neighborhood was close-knit, full of century-old Italianate row houses and scores of families whose parents and grandparents had built them. As a result, Oregon Hill has remained a vibrant urban neighborhood where people are deeply connected to one another, where the practice of neighborliness is robust and authentic.

My wife and I quickly became inculcated into this culture. We were shown by example that we were expected to participate in this way of life by doing the things neighbors have always done—sweeping the sidewalk, stopping to chat, sitting on the front porch, or joining in an impromptu neighborhood party across the street. Through these simple practices, we began to imagine a little better what Jesus might have meant when asked which was the greatest commandment. We were learning, in the streets and through our neighbors, to "love the Lord our God with all our hearts, all our souls, all our strength, and all our might, and to love our neighbors as ourselves."

Meanwhile, at the seminary, my close group of friends—we had picked up the moniker "the social justice faction," meant in a pejorative sense, but for us a badge of honor—were beginning to dream about what life might look like if we took the greatest commandment seriously. We began to recognize that the answers to our questions about justice, about wealth and poverty, and about God's abundance would have to be borne out in our lives. God had placed a serious call on our lives, and along with it a vision of how to answer that call. We started to meet on a regular basis outside of school to dream dreams, to hash out logistics, to envision a new—though really very old—way of life. We were forming a community of faith where we prayed together, sang together, ate together, and played together. We argued and shared and cried and hurt one another and learned to forgive. We recognized that through our weekly meetings, we were being called to go deeper, to uproot our lives and to give them away to the poor and to one another.

PLANTING A TREE

In this exciting, energetic period of our lives, Hyaets (pronounced /hi'-ayts/; "tree of life" in Hebrew) Community was born. We have given our lives over to answering our own questions: What if we really believe that the poor are blessed and that the kingdom of heaven belongs to them? What if we hold our goods in common and practice prayer together and invite the homeless poor into our houses? What if we really forgive a brother or sister seventy times seven? And, an even better question, why did Christians ever stop doing those things? Why has the church in America accepted bland self-help spirituality over the lifelong adventure of complete conversion? Hyaets Community is an attempt to live the adventure of conversion in the Way of Jesus.

After much discussion over the many variables about how this community would function and where, we wound up planting ourselves in Charlotte, acknowledging two essentials for ourselves: (1) that we would live with the poor and (2) that we would forge a life together. Charlotte was a new place for us, and so we needed assistance in finding a house. As we looked, we asked one question of friends, family, and other folks we got to know in the area: If you were going to move to raise a family in Charlotte, where would you *not* move to? In one memorable conversation with my aunt and uncle, longtime Charlotte residents, my uncle stated with grave concern, "You know, this is a great idea so long as you are in the right place. But there are some neighborhoods that you just don't want to go to or you'll get killed." This is exactly what I was looking for. "Will you show me where those are on this map?" I responded. Those were just the places we sought, not looking for danger, but having the conviction that those with whom we wanted to share our lives would be living in the kinds of places most people did not want to go.

Four of us moved into the same little house in the Enderly Park neighborhood of Charlotte not too long after that, stating that our purpose was to "inspire, enrich, and embody community." We spend our days learning from our neighbors and seeking to "do justice, to love mercy, and to walk humbly with God." We see injustice—neighbors living in substandard housing rented from a slippery neighborhood slumlord, violence, high rates of HIV infection, hunger, and malnutrition, and drug addictions. We also see extraordinary beauty, little glimpses of what God's kingdom might look like when it comes—dozens gathered for a cookout and backyard games, sharing our homes with the homeless, spending significant moments in tears and laughter with neighbors. We pray for that kingdom to come among and through us. We have been given great grace in our imperfect lives, and continue to seek to be good students of the poor around us in order to know more of God's grace.

We also seek to bring about justice in our little neighborhood. However, we recognize that the help offered by well-meaning middle-class white folk like us has more often than not been another form of injustice to our neighbors. We listen to our neighbors, trusting their leadership and honoring their voices. We also listen to those voices of the past that help us understand what justice looks like in the life of faith. From Martin Luther King, Jr., and St. John Chrysostom to Dorothy Day and the Desert Monastics, we listen for all the sources that can teach us how to do justice. One of the loudest of these voices comes from the prophet Amos.

AMOS'S RAIN DANCE

The cry of Amos thunders like the raging of a river: "Let justice roll down like waters / and righteousness like an ever-flowing stream" (5:24). Amos, a simple southern farm boy from the sleepy town of Tekoa, has ventured up north to announce impending doom to the government in Samaria. His message is not well received. In fact, he is accused of treason by Amaziah, the priest at Bethel, one of Israel's religious centers. Amaziah reports Amos's fiery preaching to King Jeroboam, saying, "Amos has conspired against you in the very center of the house of Israel; the land is not able to bear all his words" (7:10). Amos's words are so harsh that *the land* is unable to bear them. His preaching of God's justice and of the unrighteousness of the people, and especially the rulers, of Israel is severe enough to get him banished from the whole territory of Israel. Amaziah tells him, "O seer, go, flee away to the land of Judah, but never again prophesy at Bethel, for it is the king's sanctuary, and it is a temple for the kingdom" (7:12-13). In stating this, Amaziah nearly makes Amos's case for him. The temple that should form lives oriented to God has settled for acts of aggrandizement toward the king. The temple at Bethel has become a sanctuary for the state. Truth has been replaced with easy speech that cozies up to power, kindness has been replaced with greed, and justice has been replaced with a politics that rewards evil.

This is the setting of the book of Amos. Israel has become unfaithful to the Lord and will soon reap the consequences of the injustice and unfaithfulness they have sown. The book contains a series of oracles that seek to bring attention to the injustices that have led to Israel's coming doom and to offer an opportunity for repentance and restoration. Amos has left his flock and his sycamore trees in order to speak a word from the Lord, and he speaks it with all the power he can muster. He hardly sounds like the slow-talking southern farm boy his biographical statement says he is (7:14-15). Right in the middle of the book lies perhaps the most famous of the oracles:

> I hate, I despise your festivals,
> And I take no delight in your solemn assemblies.
> Even though you offer me your burnt offerings and grain offerings,
> I will not accept them;
> And the offerings of well-being from your fatted animals

I will not look upon.
Take away from me the noise of your songs;
I will not listen to the melody of your harps.
But let justice roll down like waters,
And righteousness like an ever-flowing stream. (5:21-24)

It is clear that God, speaking through Amos, is quite unhappy with the worship coming out of Bethel. In fact, God does not regard it as worship at all. The religious platitudes, the offerings taken at the expense of the poor, the endlessly repetitive praise songs are of no worth to God. Until justice exists within the gates, worship is a further injustice—animals are needlessly slaughtered, grain is withheld from the hungry, the noise of harp and tambourine drowns out the voices of the poor. The conclusion Amos leaves us to draw is that the doing of justice is itself an act of worship unto the living God and that short of doing justice, religious ceremonies are a mockery.

One significant issue of concern in interpreting Amos's call for justice is the need to avoid an uncritical translation of the ancient Hebrew *mishpat* as being the equivalent of the modern English word *justice*. The Hebrew term is a form of a legal word that describes the right ordering and operation of the people under the statutes that governed their interactions. It is also an attribute of God and of humans who act in fairness toward God and others. It is important to note that the *mishpat* has to do with people and the way that people treat the rest of God's creation, including other people.

Translation of the term *mishpat*, usually rendered as "justice," is tricky because it is not clear what modern Americans mean in using the word "justice." The term has become an abstraction rather than a concrete set of actions and relationships between people and with God. Today we have competing claims about justice from every side, and no common story to determine what is just and what is unjust.[1] However, the commonality that all of the competing views (e.g., liberal, conservative, libertarian, universalist, etc.) share is the notion that justice somehow has to do with making either America or the world—or both—work better. The presupposition in this way of speaking of justice is that America or the world is more determinative of our account of justice than Christianity is.[2] Christians do not believe this to be true. Rather, we believe that the good news of God as revealed in Christ Jesus and spoken through prophets like Amos is the determining factor in what we mean when we say justice. In other words, Christian claims about justice in modern or postmodern America will inevitably conflict with non-Christian claims. Christian claims of justice are determined by a particular story, one that derives meaning and inspiration from persons such as Amos, Isaiah, and Jesus, not by the goal of making America more just. America and the world may in fact become more just by the presence of justice-doing communities of Christians. This is evidence of God's work in the world, but it is not the primary task of God's people in the world.

Amos offers us several ways of understanding what God requires as it relates to justice, beginning with the second line of this verse. Amos wants us to understand justice in relation to a similar concept, righteousness. The parallelism of the verse is an undeniable link between the two concepts. In their basic Hebrew meaning, the terms are similar, but not exactly the same. Justice (*mishpat*) comes from a legal term and has to do with making a grievance right or rectifying a conflict. Both God and humans, especially judges or kings, are described as being just. The basic meaning of righteousness (*tsedeqah*) has to do with rightness, that is, things being as they should be or as God created them to be. The primary distinction between the terms is that justice carries with it a legal connotation, but righteousness extends beyond the realm of judgment-making. We might say that righteousness is a bit stronger in that no part of our lives can go untouched by it.

As it relates to Amos 5:24, the usage of the term "righteousness" takes the idea of justice and extends it beyond its typical setting in a court. This mimics the movement of the metaphor from waters to an ever-flowing stream. Rolling waters are a strong, even scary image. One can easily be swept away by a flash flood in a quick-moving wadi from a desert rainstorm. But an eternal stream is an even stronger image. It is a source of life for a desert people who experience drought and parched earth. Righteousness is a slight extension of justice here, a rhetorical heightening of God's demands for proper worship. Justice and righteousness ought to cover every aspect of life, and ought to roll down from the mountains fiercely, never to dry up.

To understand justice, Amos's prescription for Israel's salvation, we must understand righteousness. The term "righteousness" carries with it an advantage, namely that it is a term distinct to Jewish-Christian usage. The word is uncommon in the course of typical American conversation, its rare uses being in the pejorative sense regarding another person, concerning indignation, or from youth searching for a description of heavy metal bands or skateboard tricks. Unlike justice, righteousness is not complicated by multiple usages. So long as we can get past the negative connotations that Christians have come to associate with the term, it is rife with potential. Biblically the word "righteousness" simply describes right relationships from humans to other humans and between humans and God. So we might translate 5:24b to read, albeit less lyrically, "and right relationships (or rightness) like an eternal stream."

If the term "justice" suffers from lack of clarity, the term "righteousness" suffers from lack of use. Being righteous, like being holy, is out of fashion in modern America. No reasonable Christian community dares to strive for holiness or righteousness as a goal of Christian life, at least not publicly. To do so would indicate being completely out of touch with the modern world. Consequently, our imaginative resources toward envisioning what a righteous (or a holy) people might look like have been depleted.

A number of biblical sources describe what a righteous community or right relationships will look like. As we shall see, Amos himself provides a description of how the relationships among the people of Israel have been perverted, thus giving a good direction for what righteousness might look like through the repairing of those broken relationships. Before turning to that, however, another illustration of righteousness hovers, gently calling to us through Amos 5. At several points in the chapter, especially in verses 8-9 and 24, the grammar of creation dances through the text. Among the terms that echo the creation story are "made" and "makes," "destruction," that being the antithesis of creation, and the key phrase in verse 8, "who calls for the waters of the sea / and pours them out on the surface of the earth." Through the imagery of creation, the community who hears Amos's words is invited to listen not just to Amos, but also to the long faith story of God's creation and ongoing sustenance. Amos's water imagery harks back to the very story of creation in order to remind the people of who they are and of the righteousness to which they have been called.

In the story of creation, things as they are created are naturally in right relationships to God and one another. God's garden is perfect in the relationships among the plants, the earth, and the creatures. Genesis 2:5-6 states that because God had not caused rain yet, a stream would arise from the earth to water the "whole face of the ground." Genesis 2:10-14 names the rivers that flow in and through Eden. Amos's rhetoric resonates with these tales of God's creative acts. We hear in Amos's imagery of waters and an ever-flowing stream the original setting of justice and righteousness—at Eden, where all things were in right relationship with their Creator and with one another.[3]

Of course, Israel in Amos's time was a far more complicated entity than the original garden, from which humans had been absent for untold centuries. Amos provides us with the context from which to understand what the frustration of righteousness looked like in a practical sense, thus giving possibilities for remedying the injustices of the day. This context is provided throughout the book, but especially in 5:10-13. In this passage, Amos preaches through a litany of sins that have prevented justice and righteousness from thriving, including "abhorring the one who speaks truth" (v.10), trampling on and levying taxes on the poor, afflicting the righteous, taking bribes, and pushing aside the needy in the gate. This list does not encompass all of Israel's sins, instead choosing to highlight unfair decisions by judges (who heard cases at the city gates) in favor of those who can afford a bribe and practices like grain taxes that were detrimental to the poor. Amos forces Israel to look at its economic and interpersonal unrighteousness, in particular Israel's treatment of those on the margins of society. Justice and righteousness, then, look like the kind of people who will provide the poor a place to be heard, who will treat them with regard and honor. The people who can be called just or righteous will remember the kindness of God to Israel while they were poor, homeless wanderers in the desert and act out of compassion to share their grain rather than charge fees for the building of personal wealth (v. 11). The people called just and righteous will recognize in the poor their kin.

That the poor are our kin is one of the presuppositions out of which we have tried to build Hyaets Community. We see this notion as one of the basics of Christian faith—that the poor are our brothers and sisters because their story is our story. *We* were wanderers in the wilderness. *We* gathered just enough food for each day.[4] *Our* Lord had "no place to lay his head."[5] To be aliens and sojourners in any land in which we find ourselves is part of the Jewish and Christian story, but for Christians in America, and especially Baptists in the South,[6] we have traded our alien status for power in the American political system. America, for its part, has been all too accommodating to Christians willing to seek that power, thus creating a serious confusion of allegiances with many Christians.

We need the poor, and those who suffer injustice who often are the poor, to teach us how to be aliens and sojourners in our own land. Like those at Bethel and in Samaria, we Christians who are white and middle class have worshiped in the sanctuary of the powerful and have enjoyed the cozy confines of the temple of the earthly kingdom for so long that we are no longer able to recognize ourselves as the people of Israel wandering through the desert. We no longer identify ourselves completely with the one who had "no place to lay his head" (Matt 8:20). Those who suffer injustice and pay the steepest price for our unrighteousness, like Jesus, are our best teachers. If we listen to our own faith story, in the poor we know ourselves. Knowing ourselves as the poor, the alien and sojourner, we can listen better to our poor brothers and sisters who can teach us more of the truth about ourselves and about the kingdom of God.

Echoing Amos, the prophet Isaiah several hundred years later preaches a sermon to Judah similar to Amos's condemnation of Israel's religious practices:

> Look, you serve your own interest on your fast day
> And oppress all your workers. . . .
> Such fasting as you do today
> Will not make your voice heard on high. . . .
> Is not this the fast I choose:
> To loose the bonds of injustice,
> To undo the thongs of the yoke . . . ?
> Is it not to share your bread with the hungry,
> And bring the homeless poor into your house;
> When you see the naked, to cover them,
> And not to hide yourself from your own kin? (58:3b-7)

Even two centuries or more later, Isaiah states that religious practice without the establishment of righteousness within the people of God is worshiping unto our own condemnation. And further, again echoing Amos, Isaiah claims that doing justice and practicing righteousness are themselves acts of worship toward God. The same examples of unrighteousness live on in our lives today. Christians are no less guilty of oppressing workers, refusing the homeless access to our spacious houses, and serving our own interests through our religious practices than were the Israelites of Isaiah's day. As the same issues live on, so do the practical questions of how to loose the bonds of injustice and to undo the thong of the yoke.

One of the practices that Hyaets Community has found important for cultivating right relationships within the context of our neighborhood has been the sharing of meals. This is nothing groundbreaking, but it is one of the simple practices around which just communities are formed. Our friends at the Open Door Community[7] in Atlanta often say "justice is important, but supper is essential." I think they are right, and I think that at least part of what they mean is that the kinds of communities who are capable of justice and righteousness are those who sit and eat together. So we sit and eat with our neighbors. The best meals are the ones that linger, that extend out to the front porch or the horseshoe pits or to singing hymns around the piano. We share our stories, and we do this over and over until the line between guest and host becomes blurred.

We also remember in our eating that as Christians we learn what righteousness is by eating, and especially by the sacramental meal that we celebrate together. In that meal, we take our righteous and wholly just Lord into ourselves, sharing together of his body and blood. In our eating and drinking, we serve one another, we share equally, and a bit of our Lord's justice literally becomes part of us by our partaking. This supper is essential because it shows us what justice means. The righteousness of Jesus makes us brother and sister to one another, enabling us to be in right relation with all.

The two movements toward justice and righteousness, which is to say toward conversion, that I have attempted to describe here are from missionary-helper to neighbor, and from neighbor to brother or sister. Among the lessons we have learned in our community, which comes as no surprise, is that we don't always get these steps of righteousness toward the way of Jesus correct. But occasionally, we get a great glimpse of God's grace given to us as we keep striving for righteousness. One such event happened one night as I walked through the neighborhood seeking the mother of one of our boys. She was homeless at the time, moving from house to house wherever someone would let her stay. I sought her at the last house where I knew her to be.

After I knocked, a younger man answered the door and invited me in. I sensed his hesitancy, so I introduced myself and noted several other voices in the background. That seemed to make no difference, so I simply asked if I could speak with Crystal. He moved hesitantly toward the back of the house, where I had now noticed a loud shouting match going on behind a bedroom door. The man opened the door, increasing both the volume of this heated argument and the tension I noted within myself. I certainly picked a bad time. "Crystal, there is a white man at the door who wants to speak to you," he said. The tension rose again. Clearly I was unexpected and probably not welcome, either, at this point.

Before Crystal could get out of the back bedroom, our neighbor Ray popped his head around the corner. Laughing, he said, "That's not a white man. That's Greg!" Everyone in the house began laughing, me the hardest. I had been welcomed. Ray did not say it quite this way, but I know that he could have added, "He's my brother." Together, Ray and I had made one small move toward righteousness by the grace of God.

Notes

1. At least, we have no governing story that we acknowledge. But as Stanley Hauerwas has pointed out, Western modernism (as well as postmodernism) is "the story that we have no story but the story we chose when we had no story" (*Dispatches from the Front: Theological Engagements with the Secular* [Durham NC: Duke University Press] 164–76). Which is to say that even our belief that there is no common story outside of our individual self-determination is itself a narrative that governs the ways we live in the world.

2. Either that, or we are still hanging on to the last vestiges of Christendom, of the idea of making America or the world more Christian. It remains unclear to me why the story of Christianity from the period beginning with Constantine through the rise of the Moral Majority and beyond has yet to disabuse us of the notion that this is desirable, or even very Christian.

3. From a redaction-critical perspective, it is important to note that Amos is loosely structured by a later editor or editors. The thought or words of an original "Amos," or (more likely) an Amos tradition, come in short sections, typically of four to five verses. The thoughts and images still work together rhetorically, but they are not necessarily part of a unified whole, i.e., not all from a single, cohesive prophetic sermon.

4. See Deut 6:20-25. This is an important part of Israel's collective memory in retelling the story of the exodus—each successive generation is reminded of their inclusion in this story by the use of the pronouns we and us: We were Pharaoh's slaves, but the Lord brought us out of Egypt with a mighty hand, etc.

5. Matt 8:20; Luke 9:58

6. A former professor was fond of pointing out that of the three words in the name Southern Baptist Convention, "Southern" was by far the most important. Which is to say, southern-ness was (and still is in some places) more determinative of the identity of those parishioners than was being Baptist. I am southern enough myself to wonder at times whether this is really a problem.

7. http://www.opendoorcommunity.org

Chapter 9

THE JOURNEY TO CHERRY STREET

Jeanie McGowan

I planted, Apollos watered, but God gave the growth. (1 Corinthians 3:6, NRSV)

Who can know exactly when defining moments come? Mostly they take us by surprise and sometimes we don't even realize they were "defining moments" until much later.

I couldn't have been much more than eight or nine when the poorest family I ever knew moved to our southwest Missouri town and came to our Southern Baptist church. Twin girls, with crooked buckteeth and straggly hair obviously cut by their mother, didn't quite fit in with our modest but neatly dressed congregation. The girls were a little older than I, but it seemed natural to befriend them since they weren't likely to make many friends their own age. I didn't see it as a "project" to take on or a duty I needed to fulfill, but rather it came under the heading of "the right thing to do" that my mom and dad often tried to model and teach.

Soon, they invited me home with them after church one Sunday. If my mom was reluctant for me to go, I didn't notice. I did notice how terribly poor the family was when we drove up to the house. It looked like you could poke a wall with your finger and the whole thing would come tumbling down. When we stepped inside, I knew for sure they were poorer than anyone I knew. Their floors were dirt. Even my farmer grandparents, who had no indoor plumbing, at least had coverings on their floors. It was the 1950s and none of us had a lot, but we seemed positively wealthy compared to this family.

I don't remember much about that visit except that when I got home, my mom rather sheepishly told me that while she hoped I would always be friendly and kind to the girls, she also didn't want me to continue a friendship with them that might involve house visits or other visible signs of friendship. Why, they might even have lice, and what would other people think?

Now before you think my mother was some kind of terrible person, I have to tell you that she was a wonderful Christian woman whom folks often called a "prayer warrior." For all my growing-up years, she was the most powerful influence on my life as a follower of Christ. She was hard working, God fearing, and genuinely kind and compassionate. But her blind spot (and we all have them) was an exaggerated concern about what other people thought. You see, in a small town like ours, everyone knew the preachers' kids and the teachers' kids, and I was a teacher's kid. My dad brought us to Buffalo, Missouri, because he had been hired as the new principal and music teacher when I was about to enter second grade.

Buffalo was smack dab in the middle of the Missouri "Bible Belt." It was a totally "white" community with a legend that said "no black man can stay in town past sundown." With no blacks around, segregation/integration issues were nonexistent for us. We had nearly as much fear and prejudice against Catholics as other communities did against blacks. At least that's the way it was in my household.

That first defining moment when my mom asked me not to continue my friendship with the twins stayed with me a long time. It was defining for me because (1) I realized that even deeply committed Christians didn't always practice what they preached, and (2) it drove the concern about what other people thought still deeper into a little girl who wanted to please everyone.

That issue—concern about what other people thought—continued to grow within me as I matured. I knew that part of it was my feeling responsible as a Christian never to give an appearance of wrongdoing. However, even then I had a glimmer of understanding that some of it related to a lack of self-esteem and a desire to please other people even more than I desired to please God. I have often wondered what might be different had Mom not said anything to me, or had I not listened to her.

Despite that first moment of urging me not to get involved with this poor family, both my parents often encouraged me to be kind and friendly to everyone—to eat not only with my closest friends at lunch every day, but to sit with other kids, too, and to be embracing toward everyone. It was somewhat of a mixed message considering my mother's earlier guideline, but one that I understood and tried to follow.

I will say that this mixed message gave me trouble most of the time when I faced the dilemma of trying to be kind to all and yet found some who absolutely "wore me slick," as we say in Missouri. These were the folks who were so in need of attention and affirmation that they took up way too much time with their conversations. I often found myself caught between feeling a sense of compassion for them and my own thoughts of "I don't want to do this" as I listened (or tried to listen) to them go on and on. I still struggle with this.

Fast forward to the mid 1970s. My life was a full one, living in Jefferson City, Missouri, with a husband and three sons and many various church responsibilities. Other moments that changed my life came along rather frequently during those years. Meeting Ken Medema, singer-composer-artist and his wife, Jane, made a huge impact on me and started me dreaming about how I might like to live. He came to Missouri frequently at that time, and we seemed to be able to connect with him nearly every visit. I will never forget the first concert I attended of Ken's. It was electrifying for me. His words and music touched my heart as no sermon ever had. The power of his messages, through humor, deep insights, and biblical interpretation, might have been some of the first postmodern experiences that reached out and grabbed my mind—and my heart.

The Medemas lived in intentional community in New Jersey. As we got acquainted, I was fascinated with their accounts of how they voluntarily pooled their resources in order to help put one of the residents through college and to help each of them live. This was communal living at its best. Could that ever be a possibility for us?

Good friends who came into our lives modeled hospitality in the most unselfish and gracious of ways. Dear friends with only a modest income welcomed a Vietnamese refugee family into their home and housed them until they were able to find work and earn enough money to afford their own housing. Their joyful generosity both conflicted and convicted me, yet they never tried to talk others into doing the same thing or cast any guilt on those of us whose generosity was not yet so well-developed. Watching them did influence our family to develop friendships with the international students in our city. Those early friendships brought us face to face with immigration issues and how troublesome they can be.

All the compassion and conviction that I had so carefully wrapped in an acceptable package was being unwrapped in ways I could not help acknowledging. Some of the burning questions that had haunted me for years were addressed. One of the most significant questions was why evangelical Christianity and social justice were treated as if they were mutually exclusive. As I looked at Scripture, I could not find validity for choosing between one or the other, yet it seemed almost anathema for a Southern Baptist to be concerned with those "liberal causes" like hunger, poverty, civil rights, peace, justice, homelessness, and on and on.

Certain media spoke to my heart as well. Books by Keith Miller and Bruce Larson were honest about struggles we all face. These books offered a kinder, gentler face than the legalistic, judgmental sermons I had heard most of my life, and they grabbed and held my attention. I remember one author posing the question, "Why is it that folks seem to find more love and acceptance at the local bar than they do in the church?" and "Could that be why they aren't coming to our churches?" These questions made sense to me. I began reading periodicals such as "Seeds," *Faith at Work*, and *Door* (then called *Wittenberg Door*). I realized how much I enjoyed the irreverent humor that focused on the ridiculous things we Christians sometimes do in the name of God.

A few years later, after the Medemas moved to San Francisco in the Haight-Ashbury area, we listened, fascinated, to stories about their apartment building and some of the people who lived there. I remember feeling a longing welling up inside me to live in a big city where I would get to know shopkeepers by name and be salt and light in new and exciting ways—not preaching to them or targeting them to reform them, but caring about them and treating them with respect and dignity and seeing them through Jesus' eyes.

In reality, how could that ever happen? Here we were, living in the Midwest. We certainly were not in a "city" but rather a community of about 50,000. We had kids to raise and get through college and responsibilities to fulfill. In addition, my husband, Keith, seemed content with living a middle-class life where we had enough to live comfortably.

During this same time, I began yearning to attend seminary. I longed for a place that would stretch me, where I could ask and explore questions. Somewhere in the midst of this, I also struggled with a sense of God calling *me* to do something. I was spending an inordinate amount of time at the church involved in church work, so I knew it couldn't be that God wanted me to do more. No, there was something specific. But what was it?

About thirteen years ago, circumstances found me accepting a part-time position of minister for single adults. I had enjoyed working with them in

Bible studies. The single adults seemed not only to accept me but also to enjoy having me around. I realized that all my married life, God had placed around me a few single adults who became good friends and who were especially supportive and encouraging to our sons. I valued that and cherished them as friends. As I took up this new role with them, I experienced another defining moment. It is still crystal clear in my mind. I had the realization that my work with singles seemed to be what God had prepared me for all along. It was more than a "job." It was the answer to a calling, and I began a journey with these individuals that would lead to amazing places.

Soon after that, I found another dream coming true. Seminary became a reality. At seminary, I found others who had also noted a disconnect between evangelical teachings and Jesus' response to the human condition revealed in the Gospels. Peace, justice, feeding the poor, and caring for the marginalized permeated Jesus' mission and message, but they seemed under represented in our evangelical Baptist tradition. My mind and heart raced as I began to see the possibilities for weaving this message into everything I taught and did.[1]

One of my joys in the early years of my ministry with single adults was inviting some of them to join a group of us who went to a local restaurant each week after choir rehearsal. I am a social creature, so this was a natural for me. What did I hope to accomplish? First, I wanted them to know that I personally enjoyed being with them, even at when it wasn't "official ministry" time. Second, I wanted them to get to know and be known by other folks in the church. I wanted to connect them with people they might not ever meet otherwise. It worked! We soon had a table full of seven to ten people each Wednesday evening. In fact, the core of that group still meets there each week, even though some of the original folks have moved.

I began to notice that the married folks in that informal group cared about the single adults and their lives. Friendships developed, and seeing the interconnectedness of their lives was gratifying.

An outgrowth of the time I spent in this ministry is that I noticed some of my old attitudes changing. All churches have "characters"— folks who have difficulty fitting in. Sometimes poverty hinders them, sometimes it's a mental health issue, and sometimes it's a social disorder. At times I found myself wishing they weren't there. I would even feel glad when they didn't show up so I didn't have to figure out ways to try to help them feel welcome. I didn't want to feel that way, but I did. Little by little, I began to learn the difference between "tolerance" and "acceptance." I felt God changing my heart and helping me see moments of great insight or wisdom that one of them would occasionally offer.

In 2004, we moved into a beautiful, large house we built in the country. It was a dream. I had the delight of decorating it just as I wished, and it was not only lovely, but comfortable. We finally had space for all our family to gather and be in the same room when they came home. The second Christmas season we were there, we decided to do something special. We sent out elegant invitations to some of those "characters" in our church. We sent a chauffeur (my husband, Keith) to pick them up. When they arrived, they found the table beautifully decorated, place cards for each of them, and a menu printed at their plates. We served a wonderful, lavish meal and topped it off with a gift for each of them. Then it was time for the special secret of the evening, and we loaded them into our van and drove them all over town to view the Christmas lights and decorations. Listening to them *ooh* and *aah* over the wonderful sights they saw made it all worthwhile. Sharing their joy and delight in the beautiful sights was truly wonderful! It remains a highlight of the years in our lovely home.

Sometime in 2007, we headed to town one morning and I noticed a cute little brick duplex that had a "For Sale" sign outside. I said to Keith, "Gee, wish we had the money to buy that and turn it into housing for some of the young singles who come into town to work." Later that same day, I said the same thing to Melissa, our associate pastor of youth and missions. She gave me a surprised look. "Are you serious?" She then told me about a dream of hers—to live in community with other single adults. She had been looking at some properties and pondering the notion. She also wondered if she would be able to live like that, as she is an introvert who values her space and privacy.

Melissa and I drove by some of the properties she had noticed. There were several houses on Cherry Street, about six blocks from our downtown church and only a half block from the old prison site. There were two 100-year-old buildings for sale by the same owner. Tall and dignified, they were part of the historic district of Jefferson City and across the street from some lovely houses that had been restored, but they stood in a neighborhood surrounded by more rundown properties.

I have no idea how many times I drove by them before I finally got up the courage to show them to Keith. I imagined he would look at them, out of deference to me, and then acknowledge that there was no way we could/would ever consider them. Keith is an engineer by profession and is sometimes on a "slow-to-buy-into" track. He helps me, the dreamer, keep my feet on the ground and look at the practical realities of those dreams.

Imagine my surprise when he didn't seem the least big negative. (*He's just humoring me*, I thought.). I cautiously took another step and suggested we ask our real estate friend, Alan, to give us information on the properties. Alan knew all about them and wondered, as I did, why they had been on the market for so long when the positive changes in the area meant they could become a great investment. *What's wrong with them?* I wondered.

God's timing is perfect! After several months of driving by, thinking, and dreaming, we had a consultant come from Fresno, California, to work with our church one weekend. Don Simmons had bought a burned-out crack house in downtown Fresno and rehabbed it into a beautiful residence. He shared with us about how just one person moving into a neighborhood who keeps his yard clean and cut, makes the house attractive, and strives to be a good neighbor can over time influence the whole block. Then that block influences the next block, and on and on. We drove Don by our houses on Cherry Street and talked about the dream. When he returned home, he directed me to a website of folks who have done similar things so I could read about both the joys and the challenges of such an endeavor. Don was in sync with our ideas (I say "our" because Keith was becoming more involved).

We had built our beautiful large country home only four years earlier and expected to live there the rest of our lives. It was lovely, comfortable, and easy to care for and worked well for our family. It was even featured in our local newspaper with several photos of the rooms. We felt it was truly a gift from God and thus should be used to serve God, too, so it was often filled with people. We often reminded ourselves, though, that it was just a house. It was a *thing* that had no effect on who we were, and we never wanted to value it so highly that we became uncomfortable using it. It was built to make room for our eight grandchildren and our beloved dog, Maddie. No space was off limits. If something got broken or messed up, it was not a big deal.

Around this same time, an old school chum, Gary Kendall, became part of the picture. Gary is an opera singer who lives on the Upper West Side of Manhattan. He also rehabbed a civil war farmhouse in Kentucky and he has rental property in upstate New York, Kentucky, and Iowa. He had a lot of experience to share as we considered buying the Cherry Street properties. In fact, our first inquires were actually for Gary, in case he wanted to expand into Missouri. If he bought the houses (which already contained six apartments), then we would become his apartment managers. Gary was interested but not sure he wanted to commit to yet another investment.

Over a period of several months, we took the next steps. We looked at the insides of the two houses and became more enthusiastic. We explored the idea of partnering with Gary, who would also bring his experience and knowledge. We could form a limited license corporation and purchase the buildings, but the only way to do that was to sell our beautiful home. We didn't have the resources to do it any other way. We talked, prayed, and talked some more. With Gary as our partner, we found the courage to go ahead. Would our house sell in this slow market? Would the bank lend us money before we even sold the house? We were scared.

In May 2008 we purchased both buildings. The price negotiation took time, and at one point, it looked as though the sellers would not accept the top price we felt we could pay. That's when Keith put pencil to paper and figured out how we could do it. That's when I *knew* he was truly on board with the whole project. The apartments were rented and already earning income. Gary helped us begin the demolition as we fully gutted the double-apartment space we would refurbish to live in ourselves. We began the process of lining up plumbers, electricians, HVAC people, and a cabinet maker. We were our own general contractors!

The summer was long and hard. Fully tearing out the old ceiling and walls and some of the flooring took much longer than we imagined, but it was fun too. Of course, many of our friends and family thought we were crazy! That didn't bother us. We kept sight of our vision.

We garnered help wherever we could. Early on, we met R.T.,[2] an ex-con. He offered his services and worked hard alongside Keith. Grandsons, sons, a grandson-in-law, and a few others also helped get the job done. Along the way, we have encountered some wonderful surprises. R.T. had his fifty-first birthday in July. We brought a cake with his name on it and a jug of sweet tea and had a little party on the large front porch. R.T. was the guest of honor, and Victoria (a transvestite who lives three doors down) was the other guest. R.T. told us it was the first birthday cake he had ever had! We had no idea it would be his first birthday cake. He also seemed to welcome my offering a prayer of blessing on him for another new year of life. Another neighbor joined us as we partied on the porch. I remember thinking, *It feels so right! God is so good! This is exactly where we belong!*

As autumn of 2008 began, we prayed that the current financial picture of our country would not prevent us from getting our construction loan so we could begin the restoration process. We prayed that God would keep our minds clear and help us be the presence of Christ on Cherry Street. The joy of being good neighbors with the R.T.s and the Victorias of our street is immeasurable.

Yes, we will install an alarm system. Yes, we will have motion detector lights mounted outside. But, no, we will not live in fear of our neighbors. We will focus on the fact that God loves each one of them every bit as much as God loves us. We are already amazed at the richness this perspective adds to our lives. We will cherish the conversations like the one I had with a young single professional who is disillusioned by the rat race of professional advancement. He confessed that now owning his second lovely home and being single, he cannot see any purpose in moving up to yet another, larger house! He is interested in what we're doing. Who knows? He may be the next person to take a step of faith and move to his own *Cherry Street*.

At the moment, we celebrate the fact that our house sold quickly, and we have moved into a lovely, spacious apartment while we finish the house on Cherry Street. I can honestly say this is one of the best seasons of our lives. To top it off, R.T. showed up at church recently and surprised us!

We're also aware that, while our history with Cherry Street is brief, we already have incredible stories. They have confirmed to us that we are exactly where God wants us to be. They put a smile on my face every time I think of them. Our hearts are full as we revel in our opportunity and the joy it already gives us.

If you ever travel close to Jefferson City, come see us! The welcome mat is always out.

Notes

1. Working with single adults is a wonderful gift. The single community offers a wide diversity of people. There is a great wealth of talent, creativity, and leadership potential. There are also those who are socially challenged and find it difficult to fit in with others. Single adults live with much prejudice and are quite marginalized in many settings—especially churches. I cannot begin to count the number of times I've heard a single adult tell about walking into a church and feeling invisible. It wasn't that people were particularly unkind to them; they simply didn't notice the single adults.

2. The names of our neighbors have been changed to protect their privacy.

Chapter 10

LEFT OF THE DIAL

Rick Bennett

You Can Find Me Left of the Dial

Music is my lifeline. It is the lens through which I see the world. Not one to be accused of being in touch with my emotions, I use music to express them, making mixed tapes in my head and for others or lists of the greatest British one-hit wonders of the 1980s[1] if I'm bored or stressed. Yes, I am Rob Fleming from Nick Hornby's classic novel *High Fidelity*. As I write a blog posting, article for publication, or chapter in this book, I think of a song that relates to each segment, which I imagine like an album side.

The song I think of now is "Left of the Dial" by the seminal Indie band The Replacements. The song is about college radio and its underground beginnings in the noncommercial part of the FM radio dial, to the left (between 87 and 90). It is also about being a little outside the mainstream—not too far away but slightly difficult to find. That is me. Those are my thoughts. That is my faith and belief. That is why I am writing this chapter, why I care deeply about issues of social justice, and why I have been part of the emerging church movement since its inception. I am left of the dial. Here is my story.

Southern Accents

Not surprisingly, being white in a small, rural community in north Florida is beneficial. However, being a tall and abnormally skinny fourteen-year-old in north Florida is not exactly what most people call "an advantage." This is especially true when the tall, skinny, white kid spends summers working in a tobacco warehouse with larger, tougher, beefier redneck boys ready to ridicule, taunt, threaten, and occasionally inflict the latest Ric Flair wrestling moves on the skinny kid without permission.

Staring at the preternatural beard on this fifteen-year-old possible future star of a *Cops* episode, I must have realized that sticks and stones were a bit more powerful than my words.

About the time I was to become indistinguishable from a tobacco stain on the warehouse floor, Michael Perry and friend came to my rescue. I remember Michael, black and huge, saying, "Put the little white kid down." I remember this because the bullies put the little white kid down. During the ensuing negotiations, it was settled that I would be under the protectorate of the big black guys, much to my delight. This lasted for many years. I was in the midst of a scene from a bad 1980s teen flick. You know the one: teen saved by outcast, becomes best friend.

Therein was my second conversion. I was a small-town, Southern, four-teen-year-old white kid with a Rebel flag T-shirt and knowledge of Ku Klux Klan members in my church and school community who was being pro-tected from impending bullying by a couple of older, cooler, black guys who had no reason to take pity upon me.

During the next few years, this incident burned into my consciousness. As my friends made the racist jokes typical of the small-town American value system, I cringed, acutely aware of my unspoken oath to these brothers of mine. I was forced to examine my value system toward those considered "other" or outsiders in my community. While I was unaware of him at the time, I lived Miroslav Volf's theological assumption that the Christian life is a constant struggle to "embrace the other."[2] I was forced to question assump-tions and make difficult decisions. I believe my journey as a herald for God's kingdom and the desire to live justly began at that time.

I WILL FOLLOW

In Baptist vernacular, conversion happens the moment you accept Jesus as your personal Lord and Savior. There is no second conversion. There is only conversion, sanctification, and glorification. I took the classes. However, according to Brad Kallenberg, conversion is simply "change" or "repen-tance." It is my contention that we have many conversions throughout our lives, many of which are what Stanley Grenz called "life changing encounters with the Triune God which inaugurate radical breaks with our old, fallen existence and a new life in fellowship with God, other believers, and eventu-ally with all creation."[3]

My first such conversion did not happen in a Baptist church. It happened at Camp Suwannee when I was ten. In July heat in a gymnasium that stood in the woods on the banks of the Suwannee River, I left my folding chair at the invitation given by someone no older than twenty. I cried, I prayed, and I took my experience of "getting saved" as seriously as a ten-year-old can. The next week, I was baptized at First Advent Christian Church of Live Oak, Florida.

My dysfunctional relationship with Southern Baptists began the following year. My family decided to move our membership to a small Baptist church in the middle of an old cotton field. The church was dear to my mother's heart, and extended family attended there (plus, we lived in the country, so going to the city church was deemed impossible). Since I was baptized in another denomination, not of like faith (Advent Christians believe you go into a sleep state at death until the Second Coming), it was decided that I needed to be rebaptized. Even as a child who didn't understand the influence of Landmarkism on the Southern Baptist Convention, this struck me as odd.[4]

Even at a young age, I was a contrarian, looking at life through another lens, loving Jesus but questioning his church, hurt by what I saw as a lack of trust and fairness—an injustice. I was already a Christian, yet I was being told that my first baptism was not good enough.

BEST IMITATION OF MYSELF

An outsider in my own tradition, I began a life of perpetual displacement. I was a Southern Baptist who snuck over to an Episcopal church because I loved its liturgy. I burned my music albums after a Baptist revival meeting only to rebuy most of them and hide them from my friends. I was a farm boy with a subscription to *Rolling Stone*, a poor kid in the preppy crowd, with long hair and trench coat (like Johnny Bender in *The Breakfast Club*), yet well adjusted and straight as an arrow. In college, I was the Baptist Student Union kid who joined an "evil" fraternity (because I felt like God called me there). I was accepted as a Christian in the fraternity, but never as a fraternity guy by the BSU. I was the "frat guy" who respected women and convinced our fraternity to accept African-American members and a Campus Crusade for Christer who read *Sojourners* magazine. I was part of the college environmental group and marched for civil rights with Gary Hart in Forsyth, Georgia.

I spent Thursday nights at Campus Crusade for Christ meetings, then journeyed to my fraternity house for socials, followed the next morning by work at an elementary school, afternoons of volunteer work for the Earth Day festival, and maybe a rap concert at the local black college (and hopefully Saturday was game day). Always in motion, I had my foot in many worlds and a home in none.

The most significant spiritual experiences of my life during this era would have seemed unorthodox to the trained Baptist eye. I sensed the presence of God at an REM concert during my freshman year of college, standing on a club chair as Michael Stipe sang "Welcome to the Occupation" and feeling as if God were telling me, "I am even here with you." On the field at Tampa Stadium, I sang "40"[5] at the top of my lungs with everyone else in the crowd as U2 left the stage—I remember thinking, "The rocks will cry out." I marched in a civil rights parade in a racist community on Martin Luther King Jr.'s birthday. When I saw the Rocky Mountains for the first time on a college road trip, I could not understand how anyone could question God's existence. I shared the four spiritual laws with a fraternity brother in the Chapter Room during an episode of *The Simpsons*.[6] Notice that none of these things took place inside a church.

Moving on to seminary, I became the guy with a "Question Authority" bumper sticker who ended up getting a job in a traditional SBC church in Virginia, the kind that made you wear a suit on Sunday, that had one hundred International Mission Board personnel on its active attendance rolls, and that was full of money. My friends all laughed. Yet again, I was an outsider sitting inside. If I cared so deeply about the poor, the environment, and justice, how could I end up in a wealthy church ministering to rich kids concerned more about their application to the University of Virginia or William & Mary than they were about the outsiders in their schools and the global poor? I asked myself this question (along with many more) daily.

For a while I tried to fool myself: I listened to talk radio, ignored homeless people when I walked by, and did not recycle. I tried to give my students the pep talks typical of most youth ministers, and I talked about sharing Jesus without talking about justice—but it all rang hollow. This was not me. I cared about the things I tried to ignore.

In an effort to find my place again, I sought others like me. I reconnected with Evangelicals for Social Action, a local homeless ministry, and black churches in the city and even was mentored by a wise older African-American pastor who had lived his life ministering to the poor children of the projects. However, I was still dissatisfied. I was stuck once again in the chasm of competing Christian worldviews.

STUCK BETWEEN STATIONS

As you may know, a great divide happened in the Protestant Church in the early twentieth century. While the nineteenth century was filled with a double-sided gospel in which Christians were involved in sharing their faith with others and responding to the great social issues of the day—be it slavery, justice for children, or poverty—the early twentieth century brought a divide that has been bridged only lately in Evangelical circles, especially those of Southern Baptists. On one side were the Fundamentalists, concerned that followers were heading down a slippery slope of potential liberalism that would lead to denial of miracles, denial of the deity of Christ, and the destruction of the American Church. They became obsessed with the "right" beliefs and sharing those beliefs with anyone with whom they came into contact (growing the church in the meantime throughout the twentieth century).

On the other side were Charles Sheldon and Walter Rauschenbusch's so-called social gospel. Believing that the church's primary work was to bring about social change through the application of Christian ethics to the political and social spheres, this took hold in the more powerful mainline churches. The concern became with social change and societal sins at the expense of responsibility, but the churches began to see their numbers dwindle as they headed down that slippery slope with which Fundamentalists were so concerned.

Along the way, voices like those of Carl Henry and Billy Graham from both sides attempted to bridge the gap, once again bringing powerful preaching and evangelism into the same room with the social gospel and concern for the poor and oppressed. However, it was not until the 1960s and the anti-Vietnam movement that some Evangelical voices began to speak loudly enough to be heard. Taking cues from MLK, Mother Teresa, and Dorothy Day, these young thinkers laid the groundwork for the Emerging Church movement and the Evangelical church's newfound love for justice. Tom and Christine Sine, Tony Campolo, Ron Sider, and Jim Wallis had the "right" credentials and began moving the conversation toward a holistic view of the gospel, one that encompasses compassion and salvation for the entire person (the whole gospel for the whole person as it has been called), one that cares deeply about the responsibility for (and to) the individual but is concerned for the societal structures that cause many of society's ills.

While many people read *Rich Christians in an Age of Hunger* and marched against the war in Vietnam (even going as far as joining the Democratic leadership), another group of Fundamentalists and Evangelicals took the melody of the social gospel and changed the lyrics. The Religious Right was born to fight against abortion (a good thing) but also took many straightforward Republican ideas into their agenda. So, even within the Evangelical movement (and our SBCers), the same divide was once again happening.

Because of partisan thinking, which according to UVA professor Jonathan Haidt is "reject first, ask rhetorical questions later,"[7] this gap has remained for generations. Simplistically stating it, the Left side of the argument was not properly engaged on the issue of abortion, so the Right rejected the Left on poverty. The Right wanted an evangelist to tell people about Jesus at every feeding of the poor, so the Left rejected the Right's help. The Right thought any discussion of structural sin smacked of socialism, whereas the Left thought personal responsibility was a code word for doing nothing.

This dichotomy frustrated many of us growing up Baptist in the following generations. Some of my friends interested in systemic and holistic approaches to issues of justice left the Evangelical church for mainline denominations or left the church for good, while others forgot about their earlier concern for "the other" as they continued journeying deeper in the Baptist churches, leaving behind Tony Campolo for Rush Limbaugh. Those of us who stayed were subjected to accusations of socialism and liberalism, of denying the importance of evangelism, or (at worst) of being a closeted Democrat.

There was a need for systemic and holistic approaches to Christianity and justice. No longer could we feed a poor person or even teach him how to get a job. If the minimum wage was so low that he could not get an apartment, how could we be assured he would not become homeless or turn to crime? What if the homeless or poor family on welfare were victims of abuse, subjected to mental and physical violence, and unable to work because of serious psychological pain? The simplistic answers I heard lacked the compassion of Jesus and seemed to declare that accepting Jesus into one's heart would solve any problem a person had.

My Baptist brothers and sisters seemed to care about one issue of justice: abortion. It seemed to be the only place of agreement between us. But if we cared deeply for these children, shouldn't we spend as much time giving alternatives to abortion, educating women and men on contraception (if we care about saving unborn babies, should we be willing to compromise on some issues?), pushing for adoption, and creating revenue streams or jobs that would allow women to keep a baby and work as we spend protesting and trying to enact law changes? And was it good enough to be pro-life on the issue of abortion yet to care little about the environment and war? To be Whole Life, we have to be concerned with everyone who is oppressed—not only saving them from victimhood but looking at the unintended consequences of the decisions made by governments, businesses, churches, and individuals that create many of the environments in which poverty, abortion, crime, and violence flourish.

We must continue to look at the big picture, the whole system.[8] Every societal issue has causes—some of them simple, some complex, some intended, some unintended, some we can solve, and some we cannot. But these issues do not live in a vacuum. They live in complex systems that need to be studied, taken seriously, and changed on occasion. As Tony Jones tells us in *The New Christians*, those who think in this way "reject the politics and theologies of the left versus right. Seeing both sides as a remnant of modernity, they look forward to a more complex reality."[9]

I MIGHT BE WRONG

Like a fish swimming in the ocean without realizing it is in water,[10] a world with shades of grey, uncertainty, loose boundaries, and paradox is a place I am at home. My emerging faith is a faith that I have fully embraced and that embraces me. It is my skin, my lens, and my home. And while my personality as perpetual outsider makes me a good observer, I struggle as an engaged participant. Consequently, I make a great prophet and a miserable activist. I have questioned my views and beliefs (it is the natural state of emergence) and have come to understand that the Bible is the story of God dealing with a people much like me. It is a complex book with few easy answers, many paradoxes, and shades of gray throughout. It is a book that demands our attention as it stretches us, forms us into the image of God, and tells us how to follow Jesus. It should disturb us, challenge us, and shock us into being neighborly, acting justly, loving mercy, walking humbly, and doing good works in the world in which we live.

These ideas come from my heritage as a Baptist, one that believes in soul liberty, the priesthood of the believer, and the importance of every individual before God. I was taught to think by parents who questioned the assumptions of their faith; by college professors who believed in socialism, conservatism, and liberalism; and by seminary professors who dumped out our Lincoln Logs, deconstructed our faith, and taught us about Jacques Derrida, John Stuart Mill, and Karl Barth (at a conservative Baptist seminary) as well about Matthew, Mark, Luke, and John. In fact, my faith is what led me to justice and the Emergent conversation. As a Reformed Christian, I believe that while God is sovereign and all knowing, people are depraved (finite, self-centered). If we are such flawed beings, how can we ever be certain of anything beyond all doubt? This question put me on the road I now travel. On this road, I've found similar individuals, each asking similar questions, all concerned with justice (every one had been a fan of Campolo when younger), intrigued by church history and liturgy, and comfortable in the margins.

JIGSAW FALLING INTO PLACE

The playground on which I chose to work out my ideas about ministry was church planting. In 1999, my wife and I moved from Virginia to Houston to help the only other Baptist I knew who was already involved in what would become Emergent Village. Chris Seay had gathered an astonishing group of people, all wanting something different from normal church existence but not knowing the details of what it would look like. My wife was looking for deeply personal Christian community, the kind spoken of in Dietrich Bonheoffer's *Life Together* and in the second chapter of Acts, while I wanted an incubator to try crazy ideas in a safe environment. Providentially, it did not take long. The church, Ecclesia, was filled with many who, like me, longed for a more just society yet were unwilling to give up on the Baptist church.

Working with like-minded men and women, I added the word *justice* to Chris's list of values of our church. By doing this, we knew we would have to live up to it. At a Bible study one evening, one of the young men in our group, an impetuous drummer and former soccer player who had just finished reading a book on Mother Teresa, declared, "I do not want to start another group in which we just sit on our asses and talk about change, justice, and compassion. I have been part of too many of those in the church. I want us to actually get off our asses and do something!"

On that evening our group, GOYA (Get Off Your Ass), was born. We gathered a diverse group of men and women who cared about different parts of God's kingdom: a couple of rabid environmentalists; the former roommate of a missionary to orphans in India; a middle school teacher who opened his home to men on the streets; a formerly homeless man; and many others. We chose a strategy of education, inspiration, implementation, involvement, and advocacy.

Starting small, Chris afforded me the opportunity to preach sermons on environmentalism and consumerism, while the coffee became fair trade. We chose to walk individuals through social services instead of trying to do everything ourselves. Some of the time it worked out wonderfully; other times it did not. I remember the phone call I received regarding the death of a young man with many addiction issues whom I had invited to church. Months earlier we had been setting up outside for a service. This young gay man, noticeably under the influence of something stronger than Sudafed, asked what we were doing. I told him we were getting ready for church. I asked if he was interested. Growing up in the Bible Belt in churches open only to those who had already become respectable and polite members of society, I understood the sentiment behind his next words: "Is *anybody* invited?" I said, "Yes." He came and thus began his journey toward Jesus with us that evening. We poured our lives into him and he made great strides, but he never fully recovered from his addictions. I still mourn his loss, knowing he found the Love of God. I know our church was Jesus to him in his struggles (the very nature of incarnation).

After my wife and I left Ecclesia to continue our church-planting efforts in another city, Chris and the church led the greater church community in response to hurricanes, consumerism at Christmas, and ministry to those without clean water in Africa. Ecclesia has been a model of the incarnational church, opening a fair trade coffeehouse and organic cooperative for the surrounding community.

So my wife and I ventured from Houston to Boston and began a church called City on a Hill. We knew no one in the city, aside from the local Baptist group. Like a man arriving at his long, lost home for the first time, I instantly belonged in that city. No longer were my views on justice, the kingdom of God, and church outside the mainstream, except in local Baptist circles. What started as a traditional "emerging church" model quickly morphed into a banyan-tree-like conglomeration of microchurches, an intentional community in the poorest area of town, a storefront black church, and worship gatherings consisting of art, strange and beautiful music, and prophetic preaching on war/peace, the environment, poverty, genocide, sexual trafficking, and simplicity in the midst of a consumption-based society.

My stances were popular with the local Baptist church-planting strategist and director of mission. However, my lack of concern about the impending state crisis surrounding same-sex marriage along with my differing views on evangelism (non-confrontational), the War in Iraq, and alcohol put me at odds with the powers that be in my denomination.

While the national Baptist group and I were in the midst of a "trial separation," many in the local community did not trust my Baptist credentials. They assumed I was anti-alcohol, anti-gay, not interested in the poor, and concerned only about numerical growth. My love of natural foods, the environment, and all things organic led to an interesting exchange one evening between myself and a recovering Baptist couple. How could I care about such things and be Baptist? This did not make sense to them. It took a while to build trust (for them to know I was not putting them on to seem "cool"). We chose to tell people we were baptistic, emphasizing the historical understanding of Baptists with a heavy emphasis on its Anabaptist beginnings. This allowed me to explore the margins and led to strong relationships within the Black Ministerial Alliance, the Arab-American community, and with a local woman who distributed food to the poor.

While in Boston I fell under the tutelage of Doug Hall, president of the Emmanuel Gospel Center, which is an urban ministry to poor people, ethnic churches, and other groups. An expert in systems thinking who had studied under the masters at Massachusetts Institute of Technology, he opened my eyes to thinking of church, ministry, justice, family, and society as living organisms with all things dependent on the other for life. If one thing breaks down, it adversely affects the entire system. The implications for the church were huge, and we had to operate as a part of the city of Boston, not as a separate entity. I could not plant an orange tree in Boston and expect it to grow, as many had done in the past. I had to plant a tree that was indigenous to the city. The answers our church gave had to address the questions Bostonians were asking.

Therefore, we turned our attention to matters of justice, and I found my pastoral voice as a mentor (spiritual director), influencer, and prophet. A student to whom I had ministered as a youth in Virginia joined us as an intern. He radically changed our community and the city, eventually starting and pastoring a daughter congregation in the middle of the poorest neighborhood in our city and turning a former crack house into an intentional Christian community. Aaron Graham, the child of missionaries, started a group dedicated to bringing Christians in Boston together around the subject of active participation and leadership in systemic justice.

I chose to risk my position and ministry by speaking out against the invasion of Iraq, which was supported by my denomination, the month the war started. Against the better judgment of some of my elders, I drew on my childhood as the son of a veteran of three wars and addressed the historical and biblical understanding of holy war, just war, and pacifism. Simply put, this was not a just war. It was a holy war on par with the Crusades, and we were sending young men and women into harm's way to fight. I told my congregation, "You can support this if you want. Just know it is not a just war." Surprisingly, most of the congregation stayed, and people appreciated my attitude of humility and my confidence in addressing the matter. Of course, it may not have been as risky as I had feared. My church had more people who attended war protests than went to rallies for the cause (Boston is a different world).

BEAUTIFUL DAY

I am excited about the future. In my life I have seen a radical change. No longer is the message of nonviolence, the kingdom of God, justice, poverty, and a consistent ethic of life on the fringes. Brian McLaren is addressing the systems creating the crises in the world and how the church can address them with hope,[11] and people are responding. Shane Claiborne writes bestsellers. Rick Warren is addressing the issues of AIDS and peace in Africa. The Willow Creek Summits bring Bono, Catholic nuns, and Gary Haugen of the International Justice Mission as plenary speakers, while Bill Hybels addresses justice on a weekly basis. Churches throughout the nation are beginning to tire of the false dichotomy of evangelism and justice, and church leaders like Joel Hunter are greening their churches and speaking out on the need for environmental justice. (Why? Because it affects people.) Young Christian artists are singing about things besides "Jesus is my friend," and are supporting young Christian business owners who sell organic or fair trade coffee, shoes, and clothing.

Maybe I am no longer in the minority. Maybe Baptists will continue to come around. It is my hope that people of faith will understand that they lose their voices when they embed themselves in the partisan political system. The church must prophetically stand outside the political party system, as friends and critics of all leaders. It is our duty to stand for those who are unable to stand and to speak for those who are unable to speak. We are the voice for the voiceless, yet we can lose our voices when speaking out on our own behalf, especially when we feel we have grievances we must address (when society hurts our feelings). However, if the church chooses to act prophetically and incarnationally, living with and walking alongside the "other" while speaking out on his or her behalf, Mary's prayer in Luke 1 is answered. The world is turned upside down. The humble are lifted, the hungry are filled, and the rich are sent away empty. We live with hope and confidence as if the kingdom of God exists on earth, and we treat those around us accordingly, bringing that hope to them.

Everything in its Right Place

It is simple, really. Get off your ass. Start small.

As I mentioned before, I am not a purist. I am not an ideologue. I have worked in the political realm and know that hands get dirty. I know compromise is inevitable. Much of the time, we get nothing done because we are frightened that we will be impure. So we sit and wait until everything lines up perfectly. But we must start somewhere. Too often I have heard Christian friends and leaders tell me they will become involved in justice "later" or give an excuse for why they are not involved. Usually people get overwhelmed and think about or discuss and pontificate about areas of justice but do nothing.

In my latest church, I became the "justice" guy because I worked at a ministry to poor and homeless families. Instead of becoming involved with these (or any other) issues, the leadership acquiesced to me. It was my "job" to preach about poverty, justice, and anything prophetic. When some of us gathered outside a local bar one evening, a homeless woman walked up. Every other guy, including the pastor, continued with the meeting, leaning on my "expertise" as the justice guy to take care of her.

One person seated there told me, "When I move into the city, I will get involved in the city. I will start feeding the homeless. I will care about these things." Another church member shared that to simplify his life and become involved in systemic change would take a lot of effort, and, "Right now, I have a mortgage I have to take care of, so I can't be poor or live a simple life." (He will become involved, later, when he does not have so many responsibilities. Didn't Jesus address this?) The right intentions and the right theology have never helped another person. As my friend Joel says (quoting Mother Teresa), "Compassion leads to action."[12]

One of the friends I mentioned wants to start an organic garden and compost pile. I asked him why he has not done it yet. He answered that he thinks it's overwhelming. He needs to buy the right soil and the right plants, and he needs to take a class. The proper compost container is expensive, and the process is time consuming. He will try it next year. "Seriously?" I asked him. He wanted to know how my wife and I got started. I told him, "I got to know a little about it and started a pile in the back yard for compost, and my wife and I bought some soil and seeds and tilled our side yard." He responded, "That's it?" Then he wanted to know more about this and that. "Next year," I told him. "I am not trying to change the world and become the greatest organic farmer in the world. I am trying to figure it out as I go along. It will come."

When a person wants to start eating organic, should she empty her fridge and start over? No. She should buy some organic milk and see what happens. If she wants to become a person who cares about systemic, prophetic, incarnational justice, what should she do? Buy something fair trade, change to better light bulbs, read about justice, get to know someone who is in the country illegally, get to know someone poor or homeless (ask them what they need), or find all the scriptural references to poverty (there are many). Starting small is better than waiting until you can start big.

I end with this left-of-the-dial creed written by Brian McLaren for my friends Will and Lisa Samson's book *Justice in the Burbs* (a great place to start):

We believe that the living God is just
And that the true and living God loves justice.
God delights in just laws and rejoices in just people.
God sides with those who are oppressed by injustice,
And stands against oppressors.

God is grieved by unjust people and the unjust systems they create and sustain.

God blesses those who hunger and thirst for justice, and

God's kingdom belongs to those willing to be persecuted for the sake of justice.

To God, justice is a weighty thing which can never be ignored.

We believe that Jesus, the Liberating King, came to free humanity from injustice

And to display the justice of God,

In word and deed, in life, death, and resurrection.

The justice which God desires, Jesus taught, must surpass that of the hypocrites,

For the justice of God is a compassionate justice,

Rich in mercy and abounding in love

For the last, the least, the lost, and the outcast.

On his cross, Jesus drew the injustice of humanity into the light,

And there the heartless injustice of human empire met

The reconciling justice of the kingdom of God.

The resurrection of Jesus proclaims that the true justice of God,

Naked, vulnerable, and scarred by abuse, is stronger

Than the violent injustice of humanity, armed with weapons, conceit, deceit, and lies.

We believe that the Holy Spirit is here, now,

Convicting the world of sin and justice,

Warning that God's judgment will come on all that is unjust.

We believe that the Kingdom of God is justice, peace, and joy in the Holy Spirit.

Empowered by the Spirit, then, we seek first God's kingdom and God's justice,

For the world as it is has not yet become the world as God desires it to be.

And so we live, and work, and pray,

Until justice rolls down like water,

And flows strong and free like a never-failing stream.

For we believe that the living God is just

And that the true and living God loves justice.

Amen.[13]

Notes

1. Incidentally, in order, they are After the Fire's "Der Kommissar," Soft Cell's "Tainted Love," "Birds Fly (Whisper to a Scream)" by Icicle Works, "C'mon Eileen" by Dexy's Midnight Runners, "Pass the Dutchie" by Musical Youth, Gary Numan's "Cars," Thomas Dolby's "She Blinded Me with Science," "Too Shy" by Kajagoogoo, "Perfect Way" by Scritti Politti, and "Digging Your Scene" by Blow Monkeys.

2. This is one of the major themes in Miroslav Volf's theology, particularly in *Exclusion and Embrace: A Theological Exploration of Identity, Otherness, and Reconciliation* (Nashville: Abingdon, 1996).

3. Stanley J. Grenz, *Created for Community* (Grand Rapids: Baker Books, 1996) 179.

4. Although more complex than I state it, Landmarkism, which has its roots in the 1850s, sees other church traditions as invalid, especially baptism. According to this tradition, Baptists can trace their bloodlines to the first-century church.

5. In case you are not aware, "40" is the final song on the album War by U2 and is sung at the end of most of their shows. It is a reworking of Psalm 40.

6. The four spiritual laws refer to the plan of salvation espoused by Campus Crusade for Christ, and communicated through tracts as part of their evangelism strategy. An explanation of the laws can be found on the Campus Crusade website: http://www.campuscrusade.com/fourlawseng.htm.

7. Jonathan Haidt, *What Makes People Vote Republican*, at http://www.edge.org/3rd_culture/haidt08/haidt08_index.html.

8. In his book *Everything Must Change* (Nashville: Thomas Nelson, 2007), Brian McLaren addresses the major systems in crisis in the world today: the crises of the planet, poverty, peace, and purpose. The church must respond to all of these crises with hope and action. The book is unparalleled in scope and purpose in Christian publishing.

9. Tony Jones, *The New Christians* (San Francisco: Jossey Bass, 2008) 20.

10. The late David Foster Wallace made this analogy in an address to the 2005 graduating class at Kenyon College. The entire essay can be found at numerous websites, including http://www.guardian.co.uk/books/2008/sep/20/fiction.

11. Once again I recommend Brian McLaren's *Everything Must Change* for a discussion of systems thinking and how important it is for a church fully engaged in the needs of the world.

12. Joel Vestal is the founder of the missionary organization ServLife International (www.servlife.org) and author of *Dangerous Faith* (Colorado Springs: NavPress, 2007).

13. Brian McLaren, in Will and Lisa Samson, *Justice in the Burbs* (Grand Rapids: Baker Books, 2007) 31.

Chapter 11

WE WERE MADE FOR THIS

Zach Roberts

I am a suburban dad with a moderate income, two kids, and a wife who loves me in spite of my idiosyncrasies. In other words, I'm like many dudes out there, making a living and trying to be a good father and husband. I say that here at the beginning of a chapter on a "green" theological posture because caring about the planet is not the property of high-minded liberals and granola-munching tree-huggers—not that there is anything wrong with them. Ecological stewardship is the vocational responsibility of every human being.

I did not come to my convictions about the environment through the ivory towers of the university or as part of the urban trend of all things organic. I fell in love with God's green earth as a kid growing up on a ten-acre apple orchard in Monroe, Virginia, along the foothills of the Southern Appalachians. Over time, an abiding theological posture has emerged for me regarding Earth and our relationship to it, and I hope to articulate that story in this chapter.

THANKS, DAD

My dad did what many ex-hippies were doing back in the late 1970s and early 1980s. He moved his family into the country and out of the suburban nightmare. An avid reader of *Mother Earth News* and of the 1984 bestseller *Megatrends*, Dad envisioned a homestead where he could garden and get his hands dirty. A music retail store manager by day, dad became the proud farmer of an overgrown and unmaintained apple orchard on the side of Tobacco Row Mountain in Amherst County, Virginia.

I have a vivid memory of the day a pickup truck pulling a flat-bed trailer came up our gravel drive hauling a 1948 9N Ford model tractor with a "bush-hog" attachment. I got my first taste of adult freedom and responsibility on that tractor, driving it while Dad stood on a rear platform attachment spraying the trees with an organic mixture that kept the bag worms away.

The only days I spent inside were those when it rained. Our little ten-acre slice of heaven wasn't the only territory I roamed, either. The four families who lived along our gravel road all had boys my age. We would disappear for hours into the woods, building forts out of wood and brush, swinging on vines, catching crawdads in the creek, and climbing trees. We would carry our little Dorling Kindersley (DK) handbooks in our pockets to identify butterflies, insects, birds, and rocks. We were explorers in a world that fascinated us.

Dad also introduced me to what would later grow into a passion: hiking the Appalachian Trail (AT). We mostly did day hikes on various sections in Nelson County, Virginia. While we hiked, Dad quizzed me on the types of trees and plants we encountered. We ate Vienna sausages and baked beans with saltine crackers and drank Coke from a glass bottle.

Dad may not have known it at the time, but he was creating some extremely formative associations in me with the choices he made. At an early age, I understood the natural world to be a place of adventure, wonder, and friendship. It was something alive, and it gave me life. To this day, whenever I feel the need for life, I look out the window and begin to consider how to make time to wander in the woods.

MIXED SIGNALS AT CHURCH

I have been attending the Baptist church since I was in diapers. As a hyperactive kid used to roaming our land, sitting and listening at church, or anywhere else, was a bit of a challenge. I enjoyed it for the most part, but it wasn't until I got to youth group that I really began to think about life and faith. Jesus fascinated me, but church was boring. I loved youth game nights, but beyond that I found church to be too full of rules and competing egos. Like many Baptist kids, I went down and got dunked when I was thirteen. It certainly wasn't an empty ritual exercise. I wanted to follow Jesus. However, staying out of hell probably had more to do with my decision than anything.

The Bible was interesting to me, and I liked discussing and debating it whenever the opportunity arose. This sometimes got me in trouble because I would question the youth minister or my teachers. I was coming up in the faith right in the midst of the "culture wars." Ministers preached about how evil the world was, but I had my doubts. I certainly believed there were people who did bad things, but the notion that the world was inherently evil did not sit well. As an adolescent, I had no theological justification for why I disagreed with the church on the issue of the world's evilness. All I knew is that what I heard preached did not fit my experience of the world as a place of wonder and friendship. This disconnect continued to grow with me into my college years.

Hip-deep in Wolf Creek

Outside of my studies, I was committed to two things in college: soccer and fishing (at least until I met my wife . . . then there were three things). During the fall and spring, I bolted from my last class of the day and drove to Rocky Gap, Virginia, where Route 61 and I-77 intersect. There, I could be found hip-deep in Wolf Creek fishing for smallmouth, red-eye, bluegill, and rainbow trout. Most times I was alone. I felt so close to God and to what it meant to be human standing in the middle of that stream, flanked by craggy cliff sides and listening to the water pour through the rocks. I prayed, reflected, and even talked to the fish or my surroundings. I often thanked the fish before releasing them back into the water. I thanked the trees for their shade, or for the amazing color they offered in the fall. That might sound a little crazy, and only later did I discover that St. Francis was often guilty of the same "curious" behavior. I felt so connected that my talking to the fish or to my surroundings was a lot like talking to God. It was here that my prayers began to expand beyond the borders of simply kneeling and asking God for help or forgiveness.

After enjoying the freedom of being an untethered adolescent my freshman year, and finding it largely unfulfilling, I began to engage theology and the study of the Bible with a more focused intent. My framework for such an endeavor was still largely my conservative Baptist upbringing. My foray into a deeper intellectual exploration of my faith began with a brief sojourn with Calvinism and R. C. Sproul.

At first blush, I rather liked Calvinist theology, at least its conservative evangelical articulation. It was concise, rationally coherent, and it allowed me to assert myself over others in theological conversation or debate. The egocentric posture that emerged in me with my newfound "knowledge" was not lost on others, especially my family. Dad in particular pointed this out. He argued that a theology that leads to leveraging your knowledge as a way to exercise power over others doesn't seem Christ-like. That was the first crack in my Calvinist foundation. Other cracks quickly appeared as I began to compare doctrinal assumptions like "limited atonement" and "total depravity" to my own experience of the world and the God I encountered there. The God I conversed with while wading in Wolf Creek, wandering the orchard of my childhood, or hiking the AT, was not the God I experienced in Calvinism. As I began to think more critically about the person and mission of Christ, this disconnect became even greater. I quickly moved-on from the T.U.L.I.Ps, but I must credit that foray with sparking an abiding passion for rigorous theological inquiry.[1]

My fascination with Jesus and the Bible grew over my years at Bluefield College, and my engagement of the Creator through the created only deepened and expanded that passion. Toward the end of my third year in college, it became clear to me that I wanted to spend the rest of my life participating in vocational ministry. However, I was unclear about what that would be.

FROM DISILLUSIONMENT TO PILGRIMAGE

Seminary was a place of profound discoveries, not all of which were pleasant. I was a full-time student and served a church as college minister for much of my time at Southwestern Baptist Theological Seminary (SWBTS). It was no less a wilderness experience as I faced disillusionment, engaged in a critical struggle with my inherited theology, and wrestled with my own personal demons.

My first great disillusionment came by way of church history. As an undergrad history major, biblical and church history remained a concentration in my theological studies. It was here that I became more acquainted with the coercive and often cruel legacy of the church, the very narrative to which many today react when they speak disparagingly of "organized religion." Nowhere did this disappointing storyline strike closer to home than in the battle for the Southern Baptist Convention (SBC) that had raged since the 1980s. I had been clueless about this, though from time to time growing up I did hear the word "liberal" used pejoratively in church to refer to people I was encouraged not to trust.

Just a year or so prior to my arrival, SWBTS had been ground zero for a hostile exercise of power related to the battle for the SBC. Thankfully, my professor of church history, Dr. H. Leon MacBeth (who was my reason for attending SWBTS), was too tenured and too respected to be one of its victims. I found refuge in his prophetic storytelling about Baptists. Thanks to him, I was eventually able to own my Baptist identity and reconcile my disillusionment. The entire experience left me with a posture toward my tradition that was reflectively critical and unwilling to remain bound by the past. Consequently, the better part of my Baptist identity has been about imagining an alternative embodiment of it.

Part of deconstructing one's own tradition involves a critical questioning of that tradition's theology. Herein was my second great disillusionment. As I engaged in critical discourse with my theology, I also entered into a confrontation with the dark spaces of my life. Within that struggle, I realized that the church had done a good job of alienating me from a self it considered evil, but it failed to return me to wholeness. All I was ever told was to "believe," and that I needed to do so because I was unacceptable to God otherwise. What I realized is that no matter how much I thought rightly about the prescribed theological conclusions I was given, I was still broken, still empty, still largely hopeless. There was a self-contempt that my theology had not rooted out, and I knew there was no way to live the greatest commandments until that part of me had been reconciled.

Much of this would remain unresolved, only to be worked out over time as I began a long and reflective study of the Gospels and a reconstruction of my Christology. My faith's saving grace was ultimately people—my spouse, friends, and colleagues who embodied the love of God that I saw in the Jesus of the Gospels. I left seminary with a theology laid bare and a deep, abiding conviction that God was far more loving and relational than what I had understood before. Thanks to the challenges of such a wilderness journey, I had become a disciplined reader, a student of theology, and an accidental contemplative.

RESURRECTING FAITH ALONG THE MUDDY WAY

The pond was frozen solid. So much so that the swans were sitting on it, almost as if it had frozen around their legs and trapped them for the duration of the winter. With my arms full of firewood, I managed to open the door to the lodge and slip inside before it slammed behind me. The fireplace took up one entire wall of the great room. Built from the rock that makes up the Black Mountain range of western North Carolina, it was a striking piece of geological art. Among the family of campus ministers I had been adopted into, the mantle of fire-builder had been laid across my shoulders. It was a responsibility garnered by my willingness to do so and by my reputation as a backpacker. Within minutes, the cavernous fireplace was alight with the crackle of burning hardwood. It wasn't long before the room was full of warmth and conversation.

We had gathered for spiritual and professional vitalization. We had been asked to read George Hunter's *The Celtic Way of Evangelism*, and we were scheduled to participate in the practice of centering prayer. I had settled in to what would become one of the most transformative retreats of my Christian experience.

Thanks to Hunter's book, and the experience of centering prayer, a passionate quest into the Celtic tradition and contemplative practices emerged. A new arch of spiritual formation began to take shape for me personally as well as vocationally. I began to see the path of discipleship more like a rough and often treacherous trail that was fraught with challenges and adventure— what the Celtic Christians called "the muddy way." As a minister, not only was I a traveler, but I was a guide as well. This metaphor came to define my vocation, and it invigorated my own spiritual quest to articulate a theology.

Within a matrix of neomonastic introspection, theological discourse, and abiding friendship, I began re-imaging my faith and inviting others to do so with me. What had begun early in my life as a child's love for nature was finding more substantive language and practice within the Celtic and early monastic communities. As I began to engage in contemplative practices like lectio divina and centering prayer, I began to have a greater attentiveness for the present. Consequently, my theology became more focused on what was going on now and less obsessed with where I would end up when I died.

I was also rubbing against some tacit assumptions that my childhood religion attempted to stamp out or silence altogether. It wasn't until I read Stanley Grenz's *Postmodern Primer* that I realized these tacit assumptions were "postmodern." I can remember reading that book for one of my Philosophy of Religion electives and saying to myself, "This guy gets me." While the church spoke of a life with God that was fixed, unchanging, and built upon "a firm foundation," I experienced a reality that was unfixed, always changing, and liquid. I was only bothered by that when the church told me I was supposed to be. However, my comfort with complexity, uncertainty, and plurality never subsided. I felt at home in it. As I began to find myself in God through silence, lectio, and intellectual study, I began to explore the wide spaces of my postmodern assumptions and know God was present there.

Significant among those postmodern assumptions, and of utmost importance to a green theology, is the notion of interdependence. Postmodern thought did not invent interdependence. Rather, it is a revaluation of a premodern assumption that got left in the dust as civilization mechanized its modern project. Modernity produced the autonomous individual, and we see where that has taken us. My generation happened to emerge from a historical vantage point that has left us suspect of individuals and individualism, a vantage point that leads us to be concerned about how our way of life affects the lives of others and the life of our world.

This matrix of contemplative practice, theological rigor, and postmodern sensibility began to give shape to some core convictions about God, Jesus, humanity, and the Bible. A theology of ecological stewardship has emerged from these convictions.

WE WERE MADE FOR THIS

As a theologian and a minister I began building a theology, and practices, upon the postmodern/premodern assumption of interdependence rather than modern individualism. As I began to cultivate a green theology, I went first to the creation narratives in Genesis. I was reminded that on the sixth day God looked out on all that had been made and declared it good, a declaration that was never revoked after Genesis 3. This was a significant conviction among some of the desert mystics, as well as the Celtic Christians. I saw in the opening chapters of the Christian Bible a parabolic depiction of a deeply relational existence; a reality held together by mutual interdependence between God, humanity, and all creation; one in which we humans had been called *eikons*, "image-bearers"—another designation that was not revoked after chapter 3. As I explored what that meant, my theological understanding of our sacred existence began to emerge. I began to see that God had mediated a creation by granting permission through word, giving power through the Spirit (*ruach*), and entrusting the material with a response (doxology).[2] I discovered in the creation stories a rhythm of existence that honored God's character as benevolent maker, human dignity, and the thriving of all non-human creation.

Jon Levenson writes, "Two and a half millennia of Western theology have made it easy to forget that throughout the ancient Near Eastern world, including Israel, the point of creation is not the production of matter out of nothing, but rather the emergence of a stable community in a benevolent life-sustaining order."[3] Nowhere is this clearer than when one looks at the creation narratives that circulated in Mesopotamia alongside the Genesis stories.

In the Babylonian creation narrative *The Epic of Creation*, also called the *Enuma Elish*, creation happens by way of a bloody battle between Marduk and Tiamat. The world is fashioned by the victorious Marduk from the dismembered pieces of Tiamat's corpse. Humans are forged from the blood of Qingu who is put to death for leading Tiamat's army against Marduk. Humans are made to do the bidding of the gods and relegated to a life of toil and subjugation. In the *Epic of Creation* we read,

> "It was Qingu who started the war, He who incited Tiamat and gathered an army!" They bound him and held him in front of Ea, imposed the penalty on him and cut off his blood. He created mankind from his blood, imposed the toil of the gods (on man) and released the gods from it. When Ea the wise had created mankind, he imposed the toil of the gods on them—that deed is impossible to describe.[4]

Here humans are the subjects of retribution for the sins of Qingu, their source. Their existence is merely so the gods can have leisure and exercise power. This is a reflection of life in Babylon, as well as propaganda for the state that functioned like gods in reality.

The creation stories of Genesis paint quite a different picture. They weave a relational narrative wherein humanity, creation, and God depend on one another for their flourishing. Humans are not the slaves of an impetuous deity who do hard time because of the sins of their father. They are co-creators made in God's image and likeness, set to the task of blessing, sustaining, multiplying, and tending in the world they inhabit. In Genesis we read, "Then God said let us make humankind in our image, according to our likeness; and let them have dominion over the fish of the sea, and over the birds of he air, and over the cattle, and over all the wild animals of the earth, and over every creeping thing that creeps upon the earth" (Gen 1:26, NRSV).

Such an account is a significant counter-narrative. It is no wonder that the people of Israel fashioned and clung to the Genesis stories as displaced captives in lands dominated by the imperial theology of Babylon expressed in texts like the *Enuma Elish*. They would hear the *Enuma Elish* recited every year during the Babylonian New Year Festival. It was a constant reminder of their subjugation. However, in their own text, they could find a liberating existence in the high calling of being creatures made in God's image.

Those of us who read the Genesis stories today will find the same liberation. We too must struggle against a dehumanizing narrative of expressive individualism and conspicuous consumption. It is a narrative that tries to convince us that we are what we buy, and the more we have, and the newer it is, the better off we'll be. It attempts to enslave us to an ethic of making more money at all costs so we can consume with the least amount of constraint. This consumptive narrative attempts to lead us away from a co-creator's life of interdependence, stewardship, and generosity. It attempts to lead us away from being human.

This has been our struggle from the beginning. Genesis 3 is the depiction of our capacity to be led away from being human with the promise of grasping or possessing something more. What's more, such a dehumanizing movement begins with a lie about our being less than what we really are. As readers, we are privy to the fact that these characters, Adam and Eve, are made in God's likeness, which is something they don't know as participants in the plot. The serpent's appeal to them to eat the fruit assumes that they are not like God. It is an assumption they take on as well, and the rest is history. Forgetting who they are, humans suffer enmity between themselves and God, between one another, and between themselves and creation. The interdependence of the first two chapters is disrupted because humanity fails to know itself as God's beloved *eikons*.[5] God, humanity, and creation suffer because of this ignorance, which is remedied by a Galilean Jew named Jesus.

WE WERE SAVED FOR THIS

If anyone can quote a Bible verse, it is usually John 3:16. For this Gospel writer, God's love had cosmic proportions. We find throughout all four Gospels the very expression of God's faithfulness to the created: Jesus.

Jesus owns the narrative of his people and, according to the Gospel writers, fulfills it, or embodies it, and articulates a new one from it for his time. It abounds with overtures of love and admonition. His good news is cast against a backdrop of imperial subjugation and religious blindness due to self-interest, greed, and power. Like the creation narratives that informed his faith and practice, and the prophets of Israel's history, Jesus began to articulate a prophetic counter-narrative. Just as the Genesis stories of creation bumped up against the other myths of Mesopotamia, so too did Jesus' good news bump up against the good news of the Roman Empire.

Like the *Enuma Elish*, the good news of the *Pax Romana* was a violent, bloody narrative of conquest and dehumanizing power. In the midst of that came Jesus who, by his own estimation, was anointed by the Spirit of God to bring good news to the poor, proclaim release to the captives, recovery of sight to the blind, and freedom to the oppressed. Much like the picture painted in the first two chapters of Genesis, Jesus narrated, enacted, and personified God's faithfulness to the created and the high calling of humanity to bear God's image as creative stewards and partners. From the Gospels to the Epistles, one can see that Jesus is indeed the genuine *eikon*, the very thing that we fail to recognize about ourselves. His kingdom mission can be seen as a re-humanizing project—reconciling people with the image of God in which they were created.

Within an empire managed by fear and secured by the sword, such talk was seditious. The same could be said for the established religious empire of that time as well. To persist could lead to social alienation, imprisonment, or worse, death.

Jesus did persist, not just through prophetic utterance, but through signs and miracles. He persisted in healing, touching, forgiving, and reconciling. He persisted to the point of being labeled a heretic, demon-possessed, drunk, and glutton. He persisted enough to where the powers of his time became threatened, and did what worldly powers had been doing since the time of Cain. Jesus was murdered as an enemy of the state and as a threat to the established religion of his people.

From his death onward, stories and interpretations have abounded concerning the significance of his crucifixion and the veracity and implications of his resurrection. Among the many truths that inhabit such a long history of understanding and misunderstanding, of significance to a green theology today is the narrative thread of Jesus' re-humanizing mission. It is there that we are able to see ourselves as the *eikons* God made us to be. We discover the truth about ourselves when we look at Jesus: what he did and how he related to the world around him. We see it in his life lived as an expression of God's love for us, and we are able to know ourselves as creative, beloved, god-like creatures who have the capacity to bless, heal, vitalize, and give life to the world around us.

CONCLUSION

As a kid roaming our apple orchard, I felt connected to the natural world in a special way. As a child of the church, I knew that a faithful God had created it all and had given us significant responsibility to care for it. As a Baptist, I know that I have emerged from a tradition born from protest and suspicion of the status quo. I have embraced such a spirit, which is why I still identify as a Baptist. Today we need the same such spirit.

As I have listened again to the biblical texts with postmodern ears, I have discovered that ecological stewardship and earth care are the things humans were made for. One could say conversely that humans were not made to be wasteful, consumptive destroyers of the land. They are not the property of political interests. To care for something that God so loved is precisely the high calling of being human. Like our spiritual forefathers and foremothers, we must listen again to our sacred texts and inhabit the wide imaginative landscapes of God unto which they free us. From there, we must put language and flesh on new narratives for our time and place, narratives that honor the sacredness of creation and liberate humanity unto their responsibility to be image-bearing stewards of our planet. Like Jesus, the church as the now-present body of Christ is called to articulate these re-humanizing narratives drawn from the framing stories of our past.

As the church shapes and embodies these re-humanizing gospels within the countless communities and contexts where she finds herself, she will indeed forge identities that will take upon themselves the responsibilities of our interdependent existence. She will form followers who are able to shed the lies that lead us down the dehumanizing path of self-destruction, and cultivate instead a people who inhabit, engage, and bless the world around them. In the process, churches will evolve from fear-based communities of isolation and self-perpetuating exclusivism to courageous communities of world solidarity.

Notes

1. T.U.L.I.P. is a popular acronym used to describe a simplistic adaptation of the theology of John Calvin. This is also referred to as five-point Calvinism. A breakdown of the acronym can be found at the following link: http://en.wikipedia.org/wiki/Five_points_of_Calvinism#Five_points_of_Calvinism.

2. Terence Fretheim, *God and World in the Old Testament: A Relational Theology of Creation* (Nashville: Abingdon Press, 2005) 38.

3. Jon Levinson, *Creation and the Persistence of Evil* (Princeton: Princeton University Press, 1988) 12.

4. Stephanie Dally, ed., *Myths From Mesopotamia: Creation, the Flood, Gilgamesh, and Others* (New York: Oxford University Press, 1989) 261–62.

5. Scot McKnight makes use of this term in many of his writings wherein he conveys Christ's atoning work as the restoration of cracked eikons, i.e., restoring humans to their created intent as bearers of God's image. I find it useful here for many of the same reasons.

Chapter 12

I PLEDGE ALLEGIANCE TO THE KINGDOM

Amy Canosa

There are days when something happens and we know our lives will never be the same. For many of us, the events of September 11, 2001, are forever etched in our hearts and minds. I remember that day like it was yesterday. I walked out of one of my undergraduate religion courses and saw a large group of people staring at a television. When I stopped to watch, I was horrified by what I saw. A plane crashed into the first twin tower, and as the building began to collapse, people fell and jumped out of the building. It seemed unbelievable. I immediately left to try to find someone, anyone, who had not heard. I ran back to class to tell my religion professor, and then both of us made our way to a large auditorium where students were already gathering for silence and prayer. I remember feeling great sadness and pain for those who had lost their lives and their families and who continually witnessed the events for days after on television stations and in the newspapers. For weeks and months, churches were flooded with individuals seeking comfort and solace, and many people bought Bibles to seek answers for what had happened. However, in the days that followed this event, my pain and grief slowly turned to frustration and anger as I began to hear fellow Christians pray for destruction upon those who were responsible.

As the president and those in both secular and sacred leadership called the country to unite, wave flags, and pray that God would bless America again, I felt uneasy. While what happened on September 11 was tragic for the United States, these same kinds of tragedies had occurred and continue to occur in other parts of the world. Tsunamis, earthquakes, genocide, and warfare have killed thousands of people all over the world. As Christians, we have rarely acknowledged these events or even spoken a verbal prayer for the victims in our congregations. However, with the occurrence of September

11, for months and even years after this event, we are constantly reminded of our nation's tragedy.

My life and my faith changed that day. I realized that I could no longer view the United States and my citizenship in the same way. As I looked to the Scriptures and read Jesus' words in the Sermon on the Mount calling for Christians to turn the other cheek and love their enemies, I found myself at odds with what I heard our national leaders say. I began to read again about how all of humanity is made in the image of God. I recognized that the Bible does not offer exceptions when it speaks about what it means to follow Jesus. There are no phrases like "You don't have to love your enemies if . . . ." There are only commands to go the extra mile, to turn the other cheek.

In recent years, many others have also felt this tension over their citizenship. With wars continually fought by questionable means and for questionable causes and religious rhetoric a highlight of presidential campaigns in the last fifteen years, many Christians have become more engaged in questions related to church and state issues. Well-known evangelical authors have suggested we should be non-partisan, and well-known social gospelers have called us again to look at the "red letters of the Gospel" or to vote "Jesus as president." More and more, we experience a sense of uneasiness about what America demands of us as citizens as opposed to what the gospel calls us to do. How do we live in one kingdom with the realization that we are part of another kingdom? Do we simply ignore one or the other? Can we truly be in the world but not of the world? Should we try to make the United States a Christian nation, or should we ignore the government and focus our energies through the church? These questions have no easy answers, but I believe emerging Baptists are beginning to ask them and explore how to address them.

What We've Been Told

Growing up as an American and a Baptist Christian, love for God and country went hand and hand. As a young girl, I participated in GAs (Girls in Action) and other mission-oriented groups where we were constantly reminded that it was a privilege to grow up in a country that allowed us to practice our faith freely. We were told how lucky we were to have been born here, rather than in some other place like China or Russia, where we would have to hide our faith or risk dying for it. We read parts of Foxe's *Book of Martyrs* and tried to assure ourselves that if we were ever put in a position where we had to deny our faith or die, we would all gladly die for Christ. We also prayed a great deal that this would never happen and that good Christian presidents would always serve in office to assure our religious freedom.

In church we honored state holidays and recognized our veterans, celebrated our independence, and sang songs like "God Bless America" and the "Battle Hymn of the Republic." Despite the fact that I read the Bible faithfully and regularly encountered texts that suggested God's desire for me to love all people, even my enemies, it never dawned on me that Jesus might have intended me to love those whom our government referred to as communists, terrorists, and evildoers. Whenever we read Jesus' words about loving enemies, my Sunday school teacher usually made an analogy to the mean kids at school or a younger sibling that annoyed me. I was supposed to love my little brother even if he broke my toys and pulled my hair.

Alongside overt affirmations of the state in the local church, there was also a more covert affirmation of what has been called the "American Dream." People came to America in hopes of achieving this dream of health, wealth, and prosperity. The goal or dream in life was to go to a good university, marry well, find a great job with good job security, make lots of money, raise a family whose needs were met, and then retire early and explore the world. Driving this dream was a kind of "rugged individualism" that told us we could only count on ourselves to achieve it because everyone else was competing with us and there was not enough for everybody. Despite the fact that Jesus seemed to talk often of abundance, the belief in scarcity motivated us. This motivation was so powerful that it resulted in people and church communities buying into this belief, which then forced them to come up with different and new scriptural interpretations when those texts challenged their lifestyles.

When Jesus originally told the rich young ruler that he must give everything away to inherit the kingdom of God, in Sunday school we explained it away by saying we should be *willing* to give up everything for God. The vision of the church that is discussed in Acts 2 and 4 of living in community, giving extra to the needy, and having all things in common was explained away as something no longer possible in our current American context. Actually, not only was it not possible, but it sounded like the evils of communism or socialism. The teachings of Jesus had to be nuanced and compartmentalized. We found ways to fit them into our lives, as our lives were already preoccupied with achieving dreams of being independent, successful people with nice homes and perfect nuclear families. When the words of Jesus became softened and nuanced in order to fit in with the larger American culture, faith became a private matter, resulting in a personal, individualized belief system.

Somewhere along the way, my own faith in Christ became individualistic and compartmentalized. It was merely one aspect of who I was. Growing up, I saw myself as a white, middle-class, college-educated, American Christian female, and all of those parts defined me equally. My Christianity was simply one aspect of a larger list of things that held priority in my life. Despite the fact that I was told to give my whole life to Christ, what I saw practiced and modeled in churches was more like giving Jesus a seventh of my life. Jesus had Sundays, and I had every other day. The seventh left for Jesus also brought little to bear on the other parts of my life.

I had read verses that spoke of transformation taking place, of "everything becoming new" (2 Cor 5:17), but when I looked at most of the Christians around me, they did not seem all that different. They cursed less, stuck Jesus fish decals on their cars, and did not mow their lawns on Sundays, but they still wore the same brand-name clothes as everyone else, listened to the same music, engaged in heated political debates with others, and maintained the same divorce rates as non-Christians. Very little separated me from any other white, middle-class person in America.

I was first confronted with this reality while working on a college campus. One day as I sat in the student center, a young man stopped and asked me about a book I was reading for a divinity school class. As we began to talk more about Christianity and why I was going to school to be a minister, this young man unloaded many of his frustrations with the church. He had grown up in the church, but as a teenager he had wandered away. Though he was now a junior in college and extremely interested in issues related to economic sustainability and hunger and poverty, he spoke angrily about a church that did not seem to care. He told me that while he liked Jesus and thought highly of his teachings and life, he had walked away from the church because he felt they were getting Jesus wrong. He mocked Christians on campus as he saw them trying to pitch "salvation" to him while stepping over the homeless who slept on many of the roads around town. He wasn't interested in being part of a church that didn't seem interested in Jesus and who practiced a watered-down version of Jesus' teachings. He believed Jesus was a radical who called people to follow a radical dream that eventually led to peace and reconciliation. He believed in a kingdom of

God, but was unsure of who would end up in it. While on one level I grieved that such a bright, intelligent young man refused to envision a church that could change, I had to agree with him on many of his points.

As I looked at the church and myself, I began to recognize that this problem stemmed from a larger problem with discipleship. In the Baptist churches in which I grew up, discipleship actually meant evangelism. Once I became a Christian (which consisted of merely affirming that Jesus died for my sins), I became like Jesus by telling other people about Jesus. As I began to read the words of Jesus, it seemed like there was more to it. Jesus told people to deny their families, to leave their jobs, to pick up a cross and follow him. That all seemed radical to me—actually, rather impossible within the American Dream. If this was true and Jesus actually wanted Christians to do these things, it would mean living my life in a way different from what I was taught.

If in Christ, we are made new, then it means we are now free to live in the way we were intended to live, as completely reconciled with God. With this reconciliation comes a total conversion where distinctions and barriers that were thought to matter no longer do. So no longer am I a white, female, middle-class American Christian. I am a Christian who just happens to be all those other things. Being made a new creation in Christ means Christ can now be the lens through which I see the world. I am free to be and see Christ in everything I encounter. It means my purpose in life becomes realized: to be an ambassador of reconciliation in the world. As I was growing up, no one ever told me that! I was raised to work hard, love God, go to church, take care of myself, and pray for those in need. Never was it preached that it was my responsibility to help bring an end to racism or hunger or war. Yet when we read the biblical texts, we know that is what God calls us to do.

Many churches have stopped teaching about the radical call of discipleship that being a follower of Christ places on our lives. It is a change in citizenship or rather a realization of citizenship. Baptism not only represents dying to an old self and the creation of a new self; it also signals entrance into the body of Christ, a new citizenship that transcends all barriers as we know them. In Philippians, Paul says being made into a new creation means now "our citizenship is in heaven" (Phil 3:20, NRSV). We are called to be a people who must work together in order to achieve all that God has set out for us, and that is a long list. Christ has called us to carry out his mission in the world. It is a mission that involves "bringing good news to the poor, release to the captives, recovery of sight to the blind, freedom to the oppressed, and proclamation of the year of the Lord's favor" (Luke 4:18-19). It is God's mission of reconciliation. Being a citizen in God's kingdom means God gives us the opportunity to be used to bless the world.

It seems that our churches have forgotten this. Over time, we have allowed governments and culture to tell us who the church is to be and what its mission is. This is not a recent occurrence. The church has dealt with the influence of its surroundings for most of its life.

Right after the death of Jesus, it seems that the early Christians understood the radical message of Christ. They understood themselves as a part of an "*altera civitas*," an alternative community.[1] It was a community made of people from all tribes, languages, and backgrounds. The church saw itself as called out from the world in order to go back and seek God's reconciliation for it. This was not a self-exalted position where Christians found themselves better than their fellow worldly citizens, but a position ultimately that would lead to suffering and even death at the hands of worldly powers. The church's profession of Christ's lordship over the rulers and powers of the world "authorized it in and in spite of its distinctness from the world, to speak to the world in God's name, not only in evangelism but in ethical judgment as well."[2] As a result of this speaking out to the world, Christians were often martyred. They were thrown in jail and persecuted relentlessly, and yet the church grew and the good news was still spread in the world.

This changed in the fourth century when a ruler decided to become a Christian. With Constantine's openness to Christianity, Christians "fell prey to a radically realized eschatology, thus effacing most of the meaningful distinctions that it had formerly cultivated between itself and the world as distinct political societies."[3] What resulted from this conversion was an awkward alliance that ultimately silenced the church from ever speaking against the larger state powers again. This was the beginning of civil religion and the state's defining who the church was and could be and what their mission was to the world. We can be sympathetic toward these fourth-century Christians and recognize that with Constantine's leadership, they were no longer killed and persecuted. The hope had been that the state was now transformed and the gospel could spread easier and further than ever before. Often in today's culture, we hear the call for the United States to be a Christian nation and hear many Christians declaring devotion to one presidential candidate or another whom they believe to be a good Christian leader. It seems like good logic. With Constantine as leader, Christianity could spread in ways that the early Christians felt they were unable to do on their own. It seemed like a win-win situation.

Yet, when we look back on church history, we see where this system breaks down. We see crusades where millions were slaughtered for not converting to Christianity. We see Christian rulers who traveled to foreign lands where they drained the indigenous people of their resources, enslaved them, forced them to convert, and then exterminated them by force or simply through disease. We see leaders invoke the name of God for non-religious aims and use God's name in order to try to get millions of others to support their own political agendas.

In the recent election, we saw conservative Republican Christians on the Right and liberal Democratic Christians on the Left promote their favorite politicians and hail them almost as prophets of change in the world. Yet these will be the same leaders who then ask us to support the killing of thousands in other countries or promote the killing of our own in this country while Jesus' words of loving your enemies and turning the other cheek fall by the wayside or are said not to apply when it comes to patriotism.

Ultimately, the complex question remains, What does it mean to be a citizen in God's kingdom? Does it mean we must rethink our allegiance to an earthly kingdom? Does it mean we must not salute a flag that asks us to pledge allegiance to a country that chooses to do violence to people throughout the world, some of whom are our fellow Christian brothers and sisters? Do we ignore Jesus' words of releasing the captives and continue to promote practices like capital punishment? Do we ignore Christ's teachings of bringing help to the poor and food to the needy and continue to look out for ourselves and our own families while millions go hungry and die every day? Do we continue to affirm and show our patriotism to a country that in God's name drops bombs on other people?

These are the questions and the tensions that I believe emerging Christians are facing. They come not from hearts that hate the United States or think the government and the military are evil, but from people who think Jesus calls us to rethink the ways we understand kingdoms and empires. He has called us to speak truth to these institutions, not from a lofty judgmental perch, but down in the trenches with the least of these who continually find themselves oppressed by these powers. If we are called to hear and listen to the voice of the voiceless, it leads us to ask a different set of questions. An emerging vision of discipleship is a vision of citizenship that is not contained by the borders of our country. It means reclaiming our

Christian mission of providing hope to the hopeless and peace to those who need it most whoever and wherever they may be. It means loving our enemies even when they are enemies of the state. It means reclaiming God's vision for God's people, the church. We must look to Jesus, who never aligned himself with the state powers but stood over and apart from them. We too must stand apart from the state in order to speak truth to it. Clarence Jordan, a faithful Baptist father, once said, "Whenever tension ceases to exist between the church and the world, one of two things has happened: Either the world has been completely converted to Christ and his Way, or the church has watered down and compromised its original heritage."[4] If the church is to continue to be the salt and light of the world, then we must once again stand out enough for people to taste our flavor.

This means that when we hear discussions about issues such as illegal immigration, our first response is not simply to think about a loss of jobs for Americans, but perhaps to consider the people who are trying to get into this country and what their needs might be. It means not allowing ourselves to fight over whether or not women have a right to an abortion, but offering as a Christian body to raise any child that a mother wants or needs to give up. It perhaps means we think twice about the money we receive from the government for our non-profit agencies when with that money come expectations and rules about what we can and cannot say to the people to whom we minister. It means asking questions. Do we call the country's practices of teaching guerilla warfare and torture tactics to other countries through the Schools of the Americas into question? Do we as churches choose to begin to partner with one another to help kids get the attention and help they need in local public schools, or do we create our own schools and programs where discipleship can begin to be practiced and taught and lived out? Do we begin to seek alternatives for meeting the needs of the world by participating in peacekeeping teams and starting food pantries, and refusing to shop at stores that use sweatshop labor?

In my work with college students, I find more and more that this generation of students is less interested in the church and more interested in getting involved in non-profit agencies that make a difference. Some of these agencies are religious in nature, but many of them are not. As I talk with churches who are concerned about how to connect with people in their twenties and early thirties, I find myself continually telling pastors that if they want to minister to people in their twenties, then the message they preach on Sunday mornings must be a difficult one. These young people want to live for something. They want to make a difference in the world. They want to devote themselves to a cause. They need to be challenged. They want to give their lives to something worth dying for. We need their energy and passion in our churches. Jesus tells us that when we follow him, we will be persecuted. He does not say *if,* he says *when.* As citizens of the kingdom of God, we pledge our allegiance to the Triune God. As citizens, we follow in the Way of Jesus Christ, who modeled for us how we are to live in this world. As the church, we must again walk as children of God in a world fraught with nationalism, oppression, and violence. We must declare the good news of a citizenship of peace.

Notes

1. Barry Harvey, *Another City* (Harrisburg PA: Trinity Press International, 1999).

2. Ibid., 71.

3. Ibid., 72–73.

4. Clarence Jordan, *Sermon on the Mount* (Valley Forge: Judson Press, 1952) 26.

Chapter 13

FINDING SPACE TO CRITIQUE TRADITION

Perry Lee Radford

INTRODUCTION

Students of musical instruments often do not end up with their original teachers. After years of development, they transfer to other teachers who further help them refine their abilities. Rather than smothering them, this process of refinement opens up and sharpens their creativity as emerging artists. In a similar manner, the development in my own story is one of emergence from a faith tradition that I insist contains relevancies that ought to be preserved. I believe that much of the rejection Jesus experienced from his own people came from fears of losing ways of existing that they wished to preserve. We already know that Jesus did not come principally as a destroyer but rather as a fulfiller of certain laws that framed how his people lived.

The context of my spiritual development found its orientation in the coalfields of southern West Virginia. My mother was a Pentecostal woman who reared her children in the Pentecostal tradition. My father was a Baptist who reared us in the Baptist tradition. They did not flip a coin to decide which church we would attend on a given Sunday. We—at least the children—attended both churches each Sunday. There was little tension with this arrangement between my parents. The tension lay between the requirement to go to church and the desire of my siblings and me to have at least part of Sunday to go outside and play.

My father was born Baptist, bred Baptist, and died Baptist. The impact of the personal philosophies and beliefs he lived far outweighed the things he said. The example of community leadership and service he set, which I connected to his religious beliefs, spoke volumes. My father's community leadership and service did not seem contrived, but was a natural outcome of how he was wired. As public transportation was limited, several men in the community were able to work to feed their families as a result of my father's efforts. Flooding occurred frequently and bridges washed out occasionally, but in short order he was in the midst of rebuilding the bridge with the rest of the men to make sure everyone could reach the town's post office, grocery stores, and other amenities. Such examples of community involvement are needed today. They are practices that actually humanize the biblical texts that are read in our churches.

Like the music student, my journey continues to be one of development, refinement, and transference. A panoramic view of my faith odyssey reveals an African-American Baptist boy who began his journey in the coalfields of southern West Virginia and ends up as a pastor of a church that could arguably be labeled "emergent" in the Washington Metropolitan area. Running parallel to this geographical movement is the subterranean story of the spiritual emergence of a Pentecostal-Baptist who grew into many of the ideas, philosophies, and practices articulated by the Emergent Village. I often find it hard to determine whether I embraced emergent or it embraced me.

RELOCATION AND URBANIZATION

My parents' desire for expanded opportunities resulted in the all-too-common relocation and urbanization of our family. Moving from West Virginia to Washington, D.C., was a transition from which I have never fully recovered. I turned inward to get away from this strange society that I quickly learned to dislike. I emerged from my burrow to go to school and to church, the latter of which I also disliked.

My relationship with the first church I attended in D.C. was brief. Each person who entered the doors of that church was treated like a model on a runway as heads turned to scan the entering person's attire. This attention to clothing was, to me, most unacceptable in the church and turned me off to the Washington scene. African Americans have generally always dressed well when going to church. The difference was that in West Virginia, dressing up was about giving God your best and being respectable. In that particular D.C. church, it appeared to be more about dressing better than the next person. I was a poor country boy with nothing to show off, so I did not like going to church.

Our move to Washington, D.C., brought me into a new and shocking world of materialism. This new urban environment of boys and girls clubs for the youth, house parties on Friday nights, and large schools and churches placed a premium on possessions that made me anxious because I could not afford those things. Children whose parents could afford it came to school in the latest name-brand fashions. Fashions systematically came and went to keep the consumer funds flowing. A "Mr. Cool Cap," which made you a cool dude, also opened the door to the in-crowd, filled with "Chuck Taylor" tennis shoes, "Nineteens" foot apparel for girls, gabardine pants, shark-skin suits, and silk ties for church. The church there seemed to value these things too, and one's appearance had bearing on one's reception. It's not a bad thing to want to look nice and dress well, but materialism seemed to be king in my environment.

In reaction to what I saw as rampant materialism, I made a decision that ultimately nurtured the grounds for emergent seeds to grow. I determined to be a free-thinking individual. This free thinking affected my choice of friends, who were often part of society's misfits like me. It also affected the eclectic way I lived. I sang in the school choir and acted in the school plays, went outside and played basketball with roughnecks, and took weekly piano lessons. Although I sometimes paid the price of estrangement, it gave me the courage to blaze trails that felt more native to me.

The specific time and place where I made this commitment to free thinking came during the riots of 1968 when Martin Luther King, Jr., was assassinated. My family of seven lived on the upper floor of a two-bedroom apartment in a Northeast Washington ghetto. Our apartment was situated next to a large icehouse. Much of the commercial district of Northeast Washington was set ablaze, including the firehouse. Our apartment was almost engulfed in flames from the chemicals that ignited in the icehouse. Down the street, a liquor store was looted, along with the one around the corner a few blocks away. Clothing was taken from the stores. During this time, my father's community service ethic surfaced again as he joined forces with the fire department to fight the fires in the neighborhood. One famous revolutionary personality made it to my street with his "burn-baby-burn" slogan. It seemed to me as if the entire world was on fire, and while I am sure there were other volunteers, it felt as if it were just my father, his boys, and the firefighters against the world. The National Guard maintained a presence on my street, trying to quell angry residents who had become further fueled by the ingestion of looted alcohol.

A few days after the riots, the ghetto was filled with some of the best-dressed people I had ever seen in the community. I was surprised and put off when I saw this recently stolen apparel worn in the church. I wondered what kind of philosophy and religious beliefs allowed people to do what they did while professing faith in God, especially considering Dr. King's nonviolent movement. Perhaps it has something to do with what Pastor Tim Keel said in his book *Intuitive Leadership*: "Often Christians reared on the domesticated faith of Western, scientific, materialistic rationalism are the very people who are least responsive to the voice of the Spirit of God manifested through intuitive, gut-level reckoning."[1]

It made no sense to me that people could justify such behavior. I decided I could not follow that crowd, so I began blazing my own trails toward God. Even then, the grounds of emergence were being cultivated. This was the same spirit my parents had, and I was adapting it to fit my changing environment. I asked my parents if they would allow me to choose another church, and they consented.

DISCONNECT

When my parents consented, I went in search of another church. I found one filled with a membership of aging, kind, non-threatening Baptist people who seemed to model their pastor's character. I went to the early services where the associate ministers did the majority of the preaching. The ministers were kind and loving, but the sermons never made much sense to me and, consequently, I made no relevant connections to any of the issues I faced. However, this non-threatening church environment provided a place where I could move outside my burrow and still find refuge from an environment that I did not much like. It would have been great if this church actually taught the Bible in a humanizing way, especially for a boy who was entering adolescence and trying to adjust to a strange and chaotic new world. I could have spoken up and they would have heard, but I kept silent. As much as I found comfort in that particular church, it nevertheless seemed disconnected from reality and from the community that it had every opportunity to engage.

There must be some truth to the saying that "life exists on the edge of chaos." I remember when, one night during revival, a man came into the church with a bucket of guns and laid them at the altar, then stood silently. He was obviously hurting but did not seem to pose a threat. The church officers seemed puzzled. The bucket and guns disappeared, and the police came and took him away. It somehow did not seem right that no one tried to talk with him. It didn't seem right that from all our Bible studies and biblical teaching, no one could help this man. Society has many ways of expressing pain. This was one of them, and the church missed the opportunity to hurt and to heal with this man. Even back then, I dreamed of being a pastor and organizing a church where people could find new life. To me, this meant finding new hope, new love, and great friendships. I wanted to lessen the groans of a hurting world. I wanted the Bible to be more than prop.

LIFE AT SECOND BAPTIST

This desire for scriptural relevance, along with a desire for solidarity with a certain lady, attracted me to Second Baptist Church Southwest, where my foundations in Baptist doctrine were further cultivated and refined.

It was at Second Baptist that I learned what I will call "the Salvation Matrix." I had a deep desire to be "saved," but I could never figure out how to do it. No one ever explained how to do it in any of my worship experiences. I tarried for the Holy Ghost, but the only thing I felt was a deep desire to be saved because I had always heard how great it was, and I wanted a touch of greatness. Before I came to Second Baptist Church Southwest, I had asked God to come into my life one terrible night on Minnesota Avenue in Southwest Washington. He did, and I truly felt great, but somehow I did not connect that experience with being saved, so the search for God continued.

Back in West Virginia, we sat in church and no one opened the Bible to follow the preacher's sermon. I never questioned whether we should or should not do that. I assumed that there was some connection between what the preacher was saying and the Bible, but I wasn't sure what that connection was. From the Pentecostal side of my story, I knew that the shouting, the praying on one's knee for hours, the falling and rolling around on the floor under some invisible power all had something to do with wanting me to be saved, but I was never sure what I was supposed to do about it. I wanted to be saved because being saved meant I got to go to heaven. I did everything they told me to do to get saved—or at least I tried. On several occasions, I knelt down in front of the television and placed my hand on the television because the evangelist told me to do it. I did it hoping that some mysterious power would come through the TV and save me and I would know it because I would feel it, but I felt nothing. One day in Sunday school, someone asked about being saved, and the pastor explained the matrix in Romans

10:9-10. I finally understood that I had already been saved. I just didn't understand the matrix.

Armed with youthful impetuousness and excitement, I sought and secured a teaching position in the Sunday school. Afterward, I became the superintendent of the Sunday school. I organized the church's Vacation Bible School for about fifteen years. The church voted that I be trained for the board of deacons, and I received deacons' training. I became assistant to the pastor and functioned in that position for quite a while. The pastor began to feel the effects of aging, and his increasing personal responsibilities moved me closer to pastoral functions. I did all the baptisms, many of the weddings, and a majority of the weekly Bible studies. I also took on a large share of the pastoral counseling and a significant portion of the preaching for the early service.

In 1995, I graduated from Washington Bible College with an AA in Pastoral Theology and a BA in the same. From there I entered Capital Bible Seminary. In that seminary, I covered all the bases that a potential aspiring minister in a traditional church might cover. The church eventually voted that I chair the committee that would revise our Baptist constitution and bylaws. By then, I was already familiar with Baptist polity, and chairing this committee forced me to familiarize myself with a traditional church constitution and bylaws. After a couple of years of careful research and meetings with that committee, the constitution and bylaws were drafted and submitted to the pastor of the church. As one can see, my responsibilities at Second Baptist seemed to take off. As this happened, tensions began to grow within the church leadership.

The pastor, Dr. H. Joseph Franklin, is an amazing man with many talents. William Shakespeare said, "All the world's a stage," so when my portion of life's screenplay has come to a close and the credits role roll down the screen, Dr. H. Joseph Franklin's name will be among the list of credits who helped me on an amazing journey. I mentioned earlier the burrow that I crawled into to get away from a world that I did not like. Part of my distaste for that world was due to an embedded feeling of inferiority among people that I perceived as elitists. If they had money, makeup, and furs, I viewed them as elitists. By the time I met Dr. Franklin, I had followed God's leading from the deepest recesses of my burrow. I was making my first steps from that burrow back into the world from which I had withdrawn. Dr. Franklin sensed genuineness in my religious experience, took me by the hand, and pulled me into the world where I began to discover that beneath the money, makeup, and furs, people are just people.

Nevertheless, I was his assistant, and in my view—and I believe in the majority of the church's view—I was second in command to him. One of my favorite radio personalities, Dr. J. Vernon McGee, shared a teaching one time about instruments in an orchestra. None of the instruments is easy to play. They all have their difficulties. Of all the instruments to play in an orchestra, the hardest to play is second fiddle. A second fiddler must have all the skills of the first fiddler. Having the skills to play first when you are playing second is what makes it so difficult. Of course, there is the other scenario presented in an episode of my favorite television program, *The Andy Griffith Show*. Barney is tired of being the deputy, so one day Andy decides to let Barney be the sheriff, and he discovers that it is not as easy as it appears. Deputy sheriffs, vice-presidents, princes, and any other person who plays second fiddle in this life always see a better way of running the show. That was me, and there were some things I saw that I wanted to handle differently as I played second fiddle to my friend and colleague, Dr. Franklin.

WRESTLING WITH TRADITION

Empty space in the worship services was an issue of tradition that I wanted to wrestle with. Our pastor did wrestle with it. On many occasions, he stood up during the service and said, "Come on, ya'll, don't give the devil space. If God's been good to you, praise him!" However, the way he wrestled was different from the way I wanted to wrestle, and it became a source of frustration. He seemed to want to fill the space, and I wanted to cut it out. By now, I worked two jobs to feed my family, did ministerial work, and dealt with health issues. My stamina for long services was diminishing. I wanted to cut the empty spaces and consider developing a shorter worship service.

I was at a lecture at the Annual Minister's Conference and Choir Directors Guild in Hampton, Virginia, when one of the lecturers told us that Jerry Falwell had a television show (*Old Time Gospel Hour*) where he did everything in one hour. Within that hour, his choir sang two hymns; a special group sang another song; prayer was prayed; Scripture was read; he preached for thirty minutes; and he still had time to make his request for funding. Our churches take an average of two to two and a half hours to do what we do. I began to study religious programming to see how it was done. I never cared for long worship services, and I had sat in long services all my life. A church that I organized would be characterized by shorter services. Seeds for this new work were already taking shape.

I realize that the existence of "empty space" is relative because what may be empty space for some people may be significant space for others. The older generation may find relevance in things to which the younger generation cannot relate. The point is that I at least wanted to be able to engage in dialogue and wrestle with it.

Empty space has been part of God's work from the beginning. Empty spaces are created when life has run its course. A loved one departs, leaving a void. It then becomes a community responsibility to deal with the emptiness in one way or another. Whenever empty spaces appear, we have alternatives as to how to deal with them. We can allow them to remain empty and treat them as museums, or we can take empty spaces and fill them with new life. We can even bless them and move on. People shift and move to create space every day. The empty space created by the shift is part of that progress. For example, we no longer need electric typewriters. The lack of need for them is a sign of progress because we now have computers (which fill the space typewriters left behind). In our church, as in thousands of other churches, our task was to find a way to address constructively the empty spaces in worship. The course I chose was both exciting and sad. My course was to organize a new work where I could implement new ideas. It was sad because I did not want to leave the home I had found at Second Baptist, but it was time to fly.

The time approached for me to engage a new teacher for further refinement. This time the teacher would not be a person. It would be the experience of planting a new work. As I left, I took notice of the youth who seemed to be physically reacting to the traditionally long worship. They first shifted their seating in the church from the front pews to the back; then from the back to the basement; then from the basement to the churchyard. Sadly, some shifted from the churchyard to other churches. Was this shift in our youth a reaction to space that was empty for them but alive for the older generation? Was the solution for them to wait until their day came when they could create life, or had they already created life in the churchyard or somewhere else? Could it be that these youth were moving from a form of worship that they could not connect with inside the church to their own form of church outside?

Re-imagining

The generation that raised me taught me to do as I was told without question. If you questioned an adult decision, you paid a heavy price for asking. We were simply expected not to wrestle with certain things. I already knew the Lord would make a way for us, but could I at least ask how he might make that way? Could I ask what I might do while waiting for the way to be made? And what does waiting actually mean? I wanted to be able to wrestle with possible solutions to today's dilemmas. I needed a new space to do this, and I imagined that others needed the same kind of space too. Thus began "Life Step Ministries," a place and space created for people to wrestle with life's issues. At Life Step Ministries we have discovered the amazing opportunities and revelations that surface when we have room to wrestle with our questions.

In this new space, I began to examine the frameworks that shaped the traditional church to see if they were grounded in biblical principles or if they were add-ons. This framework included church music, church dogma, church idioms, and church leadership. On more than one occasion, I was confronted by those who told me what I should and should not do as a Christian. They all had litmus tests, from speaking in tongues to voting for certain presidential candidates. I was even chided for having a long face because Christians are "supposed" to smile. While I agree that there are certain expectations for Christians, I also think we need to question these expectations more often. On many occasions, Jesus, the Master Teacher, called into question the expectations and assumptions of the religious people of his day. Jesus wants us to be like him, but being made in his image and being made in the image of the church are not necessarily the same thing.

Moving Forward

Life Step Ministries encountered an issue that exists at Second Baptist and every other church. We found that our church is easy to get into but more difficult to join. I had the opportunity to visit the Lao People's Democratic Republic. While there, I realized that they wanted to see me enjoy their uniqueness. They shared their native fruit and watched me eat it with joy on their faces. They took me to the places where they worked and explained what they did. I knew they wanted me to be inspired by their work. I knew that the hospitality I encountered in Laos could be transferred to the church for seekers, where we welcome them in and allow them to enjoy our uniqueness.

Life Step Ministries' Posture

I mentioned earlier that I trained deacons for the church. By habit, I used the book that the pastor had used to train me as a deacon: *The Baptist Deacon*. I should have looked at the copyright date in the book and gotten some proper perspective. The copyright was 1955, just two years after my birth. The context of the teaching focused on training potential deacons to serve churches in 1955 rather than training deacons to serve today's church. I dealt with this relevancy gap by organizing large amounts of external material.

We often accept practice as truth without much thought, and even if we do not accept practice as truth, we often accept practices with little thought. In organizing Life Step Ministries, my reaction to these types of unquestioned frameworks has been to develop a nontraditional posture.

For example, before I organized the church, I had already grown uncomfortable with gospel music—not so much in my original church, but in the gospel world in general. Much of gospel music is very good, but as with every other art, there are framers who establish what is acceptable and not acceptable, and I am not the kind of person who gets in a box and stays there when conditions call for change. My response to the traditional limitations of gospel music was to create the "Praise Project." The purpose of the project was to move outside the established boundaries of traditional gospel, and into areas of new sound and broader language. I wanted to make a CD with a new age feel mixed with jazz. The CD was produced and published, and the project succeeded in part. I would like to have pushed the boundaries a little further, and we may go there with a sequel.

Another example of our nontraditional posture is our adaptation of the tradition of "testifying." In traditional Pentecostal and Baptist worship gatherings, testimonies are given. Many of these testimonies are predictable because of the language that has been used through the years. We don't have testimonies of this kind in Life Step. Here, people are free to testify if they want, but alternatively we have what we call "Life Moments." The "life moment" is a time when an individual shares a story from his or her life without the traditional testimony language.

Tradition has also believed that current events and sports have no place in the worship service. At Life Step, we don't believe God excludes himself from the everyday world that includes sports figures and politicians. We believe God works just as hard in these events as he does in other places.

EMERGENCE CONTINUES

One of the truest things about my emergence as a pastor has been the establishment of friendships. This speaks to the willingness of emergent thinkers to discuss, meet, and welcome new personalities in our community of seekers and ideas. I am amazed, since my story is largely one in which dialogue has been more difficult than it should have been. There are often layers of difficulty that hinder the dialogue necessary to maintain friendships while critiquing tradition. I have certainly met with those difficulties among the brethren in my tradition. I have been thoroughly refreshed by the eagerness to dialogue and welcome new personalities among emergent thinkers. I am reminded of the account of Jesus having newly recruited Matthew, who had an unpopular job, yet Jesus sat eating with him and other sinners. When the traditionalists saw it, they thought it was shameful. His willingness to dialogue with new personalities revealed talents among the outcasts that would benefit the world.

Whenever I take the Myers Briggs personality test, I always test introverted. Yet, I am an introvert who has learned to reach out and dialogue, especially when there is space for it. From the perspective of one who used to burrow inward to get away from a world he did not like, this is exhilarating. I have found a home among emergents because of the space within the movement to dialogue about new visions of the church.

Note

1. Tim Keel, *Intuitive Leadership* (Grand Rapids: Baker Books, 2007) 260.

THERE AND BACK AGAIN

Tim Conder

I grew up in a rural Southern Baptist church whose long suits were generosity, hospitality, a fervent pietism that challenged all who would listen to "get right with God," a love of traditions from bygone eras, and a commiserate heavy dose of good ol' fashioned cultural conservatism with the explicit goal of protecting a way of life that seemed to be disappearing in the wake of urban encroachment. But one could do a whole lot worse. I will always value the myriad lessons of shared friendship, joy, or grief and the inexhaustible willingness to be inconvenienced for the sake of love of neighbor.

But one obvious short suit was theological reflection. The whole enterprise of theological exploration sounded a lot like foreplay to the kind of changes we so desperately sought to avoid or even prevent. When I realized that Bible studies and sermons were highly saturated in certainties and admonitions and seemingly allergic to dialogue about my expanding theological and cultural questions, I began to turn to my inquisitiveness and attention to "outside sources."

One of those extracurricular sources was the bold theological imagination of J. R. R. Tolkien. Reading *The Hobbit* in the ninth grade, I found both the fantastical characters and the grand themes delightful vessels for my wonderings and wanderings. Bilbo Baggins, the chubby, seed cake loving, woolly-footed hero came up with his own unwieldy title for the great history in which he lived: "My Diary. My Unexpected Journey. There and Back Again. And What Happened After." His personal journey was from the familiarity, comfort, and safety of home to face grave danger and conflict only to return home again. There and back again. But he did not return home unchanged. As he approached the gentle lands of his home, where he "had been born and bred, where the shapes of the land and of the trees were as well known to him as his hands and toes," Bilbo recited a self-composed song about the road where global visions collided with the simple joys of home.[1] Bilbo could have never constructed this simple and beautiful verse without the experiences of his adventure. Gandalf, wizard and wise mentor, retorted, "My dear Bilbo! . . . Something is the matter with you! You are not the hobbit that you were."[2] Among the many theological lessons I learned at the pen of Tolkien, not the least was the value and role of journey in the transformations in persons and communities.

The Bible has its own grand story of "there and back again" that surely Tolkien, a faithful Christian, would have known. This epic is the story of Jacob, the son of Isaac and grandson of Abraham, which fills nearly one third of the book of Genesis and is longer than many of the other books of the Bible.

Like Bilbo, Jacob is a man who loved the comforts of home and is more than a bit of a burglar, having stolen the birthright and blessing of his older brother, Esau. His journey from home includes tragedy, treachery, and the gathering of a fortune (again like Bilbo). Early in his flight, at a place he later names "Bethel," he has a grand vision of God's presence but does not recognize it or appreciate it in the moment. Jacob laments, "'Surely the LORD is in this place, and I was not aware of it. . . . How awesome is this place! This is none other than the house of God; this is the gate of heaven'" (Gen 28:16-17). After a fateful series of marriages and the treachery of his kinsman and father-in-law, Laban, Jacob begins his long road home. It is quite clear from the story that he is returning to Bethel, the place where he saw God. On the way to Bethel, in a bizarre scene of wrestling, begging, and injury, Jacob finally accepts the blessing that God had been trying to give him throughout his life. The very next day, he meets Esau, the brother he wronged. Instead of a bloody fight, Jacob encounters forgiveness, reconciliation, and the restoration of his family.

Like Bilbo, Jacob returned home from "there" an entirely changed man. The swindler and bargainer became a man of integrity who is defined by his relationships rather than his property. The one who doubted God's blessing received it with open arms. The memorial he erected in Bethel, his new dwelling place, was a marker not only to the graciousness of God, but also a reflection on his growth, the reconciliation and blessing he experienced, and the future these gifts promised.

When I read this manuscript, I thought immediately of Bilbo, Jacob, and metanarratives of departure, return, and transformation. Some of the writers of this volume are dear friends and others I have just met by reading their stories. They share with us a largely common story—a journey to new spaces, practices, or thoughts from a common Baptist heritage and a return to this community as heralds (of new possibilities and new horizons), prophets (seeing current realities or historical traditions from a new lens), poets (bringing new words of meaning to the story of a collective faith tradition), or simple sojourners (with a story to share with any who will listen).

Some of their returns are gentle re-emergences. Mike Gregg and Wes Hunter's essays on worship are certainly in this tone. Their "return" asks us to consider new lands while also strongly affirming our ancestral "home" in worship styles and traditions. Cathy Payne Anderson offers a warm invitation to the joy of ancient, well-traveled roads of prayer practices and spiritual formation. Her "journey away" is actually *to* a home that many of us have long forgotten. Christina Whitehouse-Suggs directs our attention to the center of home spaces—the table and its inspiration of the practice of hospitality. Her vulnerable words and personal story cuts in every direction on a linear time scale, remembering the historical practice of the church and beckoning us to a new space where our relational interactions are fully shaped by hospitality. But don't be fooled by her kindness, vulnerability, and gentle imagination. I believe, and have written in books of my own, that hospitality is perhaps the most critical act of spiritual formation, a discipline that shapes all other disciplines. Christina knows this. Hospitality is a dangerous practice that will transform not just our faith impulses but also every boundary that we've created. The table that she describes redefines all of our notions of home, safety, and our identities as the children of God. (If I've inspired you to read again the Jacob story, read carefully the horrific narrative in Genesis 34. This story portrays what happens when the hospitality is lost, both in the treatment of Dinah by the Shechemites and the murderous opportunism of her brothers.)

Some of these stories take a more prophetic tone of urgency and alarm. These travelers tell us, in a manner, that we had better get on the road fast, or there will be hell to pay. Old friends of mine, Tripp Fuller and Rick Bennett, embody this alarm by telling us the time is now (Tripp) and get "off your ass" (Rick)! Tripp tells us to join in the "Abba" movement of hope. Repent. Believe. The time is now for the church to shed its Western, colonial "chains" and embrace something far larger, living in anticipation for a new order and time of re-creation, restoration, healing, and intimacy. Rick is equally concerned about our reductions of the gospel. He reminds us that a passion for justice and restoration of all of God's creation is not an advanced course for the especially motivated or an elective to be taken if time allows after the core curriculum is fulfilled. This passion is the core curriculum, not an activity to be engaged conveniently when time, life status, or resources allow. Another friend, Amy Canosa, raises an issue of allegiance. Whose flag do we carry as we journey, that of our nation or the banner of the triune God? The sentimentalities and entanglements of our social histories, ethnicities, denominations, and nations can obscure the true breadth of the transformation and reconciliation available on the journey. Our nationalism and other such allegiances tell us that we're "there" when we've only become to travel or that we're "home" when we're many leagues away from God's vision for our community life.

The great journey narratives typically maintain a defensive and loving posture in regards to "home," even when that which represents home is being critiqued or challenged to change. These essays all shared a loving perspective toward the Baptist tradition. As I wrote earlier, we could have all done a lot worse. Epic journey stories also are typically catalyzed by threats— distant or near, external or internal. Bilbo's story was not just about the ease of his life at home or the deep-rooted strength of a small people who cherished the simple wonders of family, friendship, agriculture, hearty fare, multiple breakfasts(!), and the blessed mundane. There were growing whispers of a stirring evil and that would threaten even the most inconsequential and isolated communities. In these essays, we've heard some whispers and some exclamations of threat. Excessive individualism, blind nationalism, petrified traditionalism, unchecked consumerism, and many other descriptions of a constricted gospel have been exposed as threats to the contemporary church.

But as was the case with Bilbo and the Bible's Jacob, home and threats serve as foreground and background in stories that are devoted to new horizons and vital transformation. In case of the Bible, the true hero of the story is always God. The human protagonists are always foils, noble and less so (like Jacob), to the gracious action of a redeeming and loving God. The story is inevitably embedded with an invitation, a beckoning to embrace a new horizon or a new manifestation or possibility of God's redemptive work. In Jacob's case, he simply needed to let go of the moribund notion that he needed to secure his own good fortune and rest in the promise made earlier and repeated often that God would not only bless him, but also bless the world in the family he was forming around Jacob.

This book has been, above all other descriptions, a grand invitation to new horizons of change that will bless a beloved tradition in a season of uncertainty and possibility. The invitation has been framed in recommendations to both reclaim the past and to step boldly into a new future by the medium of passionate, personal narratives. In all of these stories, the creating and redeeming God has claimed that role as "hero." Yahweh, "Abba," remains the instigator of transformation, an effusive parent welcoming home adventurous daughters and sons.

When I was a first semester seminary student in 1983, I somehow found my way into an upper level class taught by an acclaimed scholar on the dynamics of spiritual formation and social change in the contemporary church. I nervously submitted the following thesis for a semester-long paper that would determine my grade: "Are Southern Baptists Evangelicals?" The professor practically leapt from his podium when he saw my thesis statement stating openly that was by far "the most important question" being raised in the current class and that he would read my work eagerly (to my horror!—so much for staying under the radar). Those were the days in the recent aftermath of the inerrancy wars, Harold Lindsell's *Battle for the Bible,* and a long delayed seismic shift in the vast, seemingly homogenous Southern Baptist Convention. The fundamentalist/modernist schism, which divided Protestant denominations far earlier in the century, had germinated slowly and below the surface in the nation's largest denomination due to regional identity. In other words, it had meant more to be Southern than to hash out theological differences in light of, as my grandmother used to say, "the recent unpleasantness" (meaning the Civil War!). But theological diversities could no longer be hidden under the bushel of regionalism. Southern Baptists conservatives and moderates were marching out into open war. Huge questions boiled to surface. For some the question was denominational, "What truly is a Baptist?" For conservatives particularly, the question became "What are the essentials that one must claim to be trusted as an Evangelical?"

Neither of these questions has been even remotely resolved. Struggles of division are still quite evident among Baptists. Seemingly every year, a national campus ministry, a political organization, or high profile pastors have either had to defend their "evangelicalism" or have gone on the offensive to root out those who have let the banner slip. But, in the ensuing twenty-five years since my first seminary paper, while these theological battles are still being fought, at least the "threat" behind the whispers has emerged. Some call that threat "postmodernity" and its philosophical maze of preferences, conflicting local stories, and the absence of universal truths. Others prefer to use the language of "post-Christianity," delighting in or lamenting in a growing pluralism where Judeo-Christian ethics and explanations no longer dominate the social, intellectual, political, and ethical land-scape of our society. Regardless of one's language or one's bias in the current culture wars, many would agree that seismic change is occurring. The land-scape and cultural context have changed profoundly.

One of my greatest joys in reading these authentic and passionate essays is that they do not dwell on weary and tangential questions such as the iden-tity of true Baptists, true liberals, or true evangelicals. While always being respectful (and honest) about past traditions, this collection of stories is con-stantly straining toward new horizons of meaning, gospel, and redemptive possibility. These narratives represent people who are thankfully changing the question from "Who are we as compared to some generally defined other?" to "Who can we become in this new cultural landscape?" and "How can the gospel of grace and redemption be more clearly perceived and more abundantly embodied in this new world of possibility?" In this way, they take us there, somewhere else, and yet bring us home again, for God's redemptive project has always been our true home and destination. When we accept the invitations of these stories, the invitation to adventure, we go home as changed persons and changed communities. We are not what we once were. This is indeed "gospel," good news. Zach Roberts's chorus rever-berates with us, "We were made for this."

Notes

1. J. R. R. Tolkien, *The Return of the King* (Boston: Houghton Mifflin, 1965) 307.
2. J. R. R. Tolkien, *The Hobbit* (Boston: Houghton Mifflin, 1966) 312–13.

ABOUT THE CONTRIBUTORS

Name: George (Tripp) Fuller III
Hometown: Raleigh, North Carolina
Current Home: Redondo Beach, California
College: Campbell University, 2004
Seminary/Divinity School: Wake Forest University Divinity School, 2007; Claremont Graduate University, 2012
Blog: http://homebrewedchristianity.com

Favorite Activities: reading, blogging, podcasting, playing guitar, and watching Dodger games with Elgin

Interests: Philosophical theology, cigars, Shaq, song writing, and attempting to be romantic

About Me: An ordained Baptist minister (married to another Baptist minister), I am the beautiful mixture of a preacher's and teacher's kid. My wife, Alecia, and I have been married seven years and have an awesome baby boy named Elgin Thomas Fuller (aka E.T.). We share a single Christian education position in California while I am working on my PhD in Constructive Christian Theology at Claremont Graduate University. Living on the beach has its perks, and we really love them.

Name: Ed Cyzewski
Hometown: Philadelphia, Pennsylvania
Current Home: Storrs, Connecticut
College: Taylor University, 2001
Seminary/Divinity School: Biblical Theological Seminary, 2005
Blog: http://www.inamirrordimly.com and www.edcyz.com

Favorite Activities: Hiking, kayaking, gardening, writing, and reading (hopefully doing most of those at Lake George in New York)

Interests: My interests include the interaction of Christian theology and culture, the publishing industry, helping new writers get published, online social media, blogging, and reading personal narrative. I'm committed to progressive evangelical Christianity and holding on to what is best from my Baptist roots.

About Me: I am a writer and speaker who publishes books, writes articles, blogs often, and gives seminars on theology and writing/publishing. My publications include *Coffeehouse Theology: Reflecting on God in Everyday Life, The Coffeehouse Theology Bible Study Guide,* and *The Coffeehouse Theology Contemporary Issues Discussion Guide.*

Name: Michael Raimer-Goodman
Hometown: Raleigh, North Carolina
Current Home: Houston, Texas
College: Campbell University, 2004
Seminary/Divinity School: Candler School of Theology at Emory University, 2007
Blog: http://goodmanmusings.blogspot.com

Favorite Activities: Singing, dancing, cooking, reading, chasing sunsets, traveling, listening, sitting, cycling, ultimate Frisbee, mourning, celebrating, emptying, filling, making a documentary, watching movies, breaking out, breaking through, watching children play, playing like a child, writing, finding the profound in the mundane, experiencing life and all its fullness, experiencing love and all its heartache, tickling the ivories, being with my wife, inquiring about Jesus, searching for the Spirit and being found

Interests: My spectacular wife, Lauren; my silly dog, Bruce; good beer; the occasional hookah; internal spelunking; friends; music; politics of power and glorious regime changes in the direction of God's Lovedom; books that critically engage; hard work that brings reconciliation; deep audacious hope; big ideas; courageous questions; the members of the Trinity; chocolate covered strawberries

About Me: If there's a dance going on, I want to join it. If there's a song to be heard, I want to feel it. I do stop to smell the roses, most of the time. I once picked up a rock because it was shaped and colored differently than those around it. I have it on my desk. It's pretty. The facts of life and consciousness still amaze me. I still feel small when I stand beside the ocean, but not because the song told me to . . . it's a really big ocean. I'm currently writing my first book. It's about how crazy Love is. I have yet to pick a publisher.

Name: Mike Gregg
Hometown: Nashville, Tennessee
Current Home: Atlanta, Georgia

College: Belmont University, 2001
Seminary/Divinity School: Wake Forest University Divinity School, 2004
Blog: http://unchartedfuture.blogspot.com/

Favorite Activities: Working out at the Y, yoga, hunting in South Georgia, riding in my Jeep, consuming way too much candy, writing every now and then

Interests: I love anything Mac or Apple, watching baseball and playing fantasy baseball, beginner graphic designing, J. Crew clothing, Junior Mints, and scary movies.

About Me: I am enjoying this fun messiness called life. I adore my wife, Amanda, and love hanging out with my beagle, Gracie. I tend to be a clean freak and have an organizational system for everything. I love to eat spicy foods at every meal, including breakfast if I get a chance. I think I might watch too much television if I could ever get my nose out of my laptop. I might be too nice of a person but I would rather err on the side of pleasantness than nastiness.

Name: Wanda Kidd
Hometown: grew up in Hillsborough, North Carolina
Current Home: Cullowhee, North Carolina
College: Western Carolina University, 1976
Seminary/Divinity School: Southeastern Baptist Theological, 1985; Drew Divinity School, 2001
Favorite Activity: Travel

Interest: Jewelry making

About Me: I have a passion for students and campus ministry. There is a need to help build bridges between young adults, their call to serve Christ and helping them to find their place and voice to serve. I am married to Dan Kidd and have a grown son and daughter.

Name: Cathy Payne Anderson
Hometown: "The South"
Current Home: Kennesaw, Georgia
College: Carson-Newman College, 1988
Seminary/Divinity School: The Southern Baptist Theological Seminary, 1994

Favorite Activities: Hanging with family, reading, crocheting, using Facebook, making music, writing

Interests: Children and worship, labyrinth walking, camping, tennis (watching, not playing)

About Me: I am a mom, wife, daughter, sister, minister, friend, chaplain, pet owner, and lover of Facebook (and I'm tired a lot of the time). In fall 2009 I transitioned from local church ministry (where I had been for more than twenty years) to hospital ministry (where my heart is now). My life is filled with really good friends—the dearest being my sweet husband, Bruce. I am a beloved child of God, and when I stop to remember that truth, I am still surprised and overwhelmed.

Name: Christina Whitehouse-Suggs
Hometown: Miami, Florida
Current Home: Columbia, South Carolina
College: Gardner-Webb University, 1999
Seminary/Divinity School: Campbell University Divinity School, 2007
Blog: http://cwsuggs.livejournal.com

Favorite Activities: Yoga, lounging in the sun, playing volleyball, sleeping

Interests: Theater, singing, reading, cooking, theology

About Me: I am a chameleon who struggles with finding a color of my own. I am a performer who often loses her voice only to find it in silence. I am a minister who is more comfortable among sinners than saints.

Name: Greg Jarrell
Hometown: Fuquay-Varina, North Carolina
Current Home: Charlotte, North Carolina
College: Appalachian State University, 2000
Seminary/Divinity School: Baptist Theological Seminary at Richmond, 2005

Favorite Activities: Hanging with Helms and John Tyson, playing jazz, basketball, baseball, cooking, gardening, reading, playing horseshoes with neighbors, cycling, front porch conversations, dreaming, writing, sitting still

Interests: Simplicity, peacemaking, urbanism, architecture, John Coltrane, Bela Bartok, Sonny Rollins, Bill Evans, Miles Davis, Charlie Parker, Stravinsky, Duke Ellington, Karl Barth, Stanley Hauerwas, Wendell Berry, urban gardening, local food, Duke basketball, monasticism, Mitch Hedberg, reconciliation, justice, hospitality, baseball

About Me: I am co-founder of Hyaets ("tree of life") Community, a Christian community of hospitality in west Charlotte. We covenant to share our lives with one another and with our neighbors in an effort to embody and to witness to God's peaceable kingdom.

I love to laugh. I also enjoy hanging out with my wife, Helms, and my son, John Tyson; reading almost anything; and pitching horseshoes with neighbors, which I think may be the contemplative's perfect game. I currently serve as chaplain with the Regional AIDS Interfaith Network, and also work as a saxophonist around Charlotte, having had the privilege of performing with many local groups and a few nationally-known artists, including Natalie Cole, Manhattan Transfer, the Four Tops, and the Temptations. I am widely feared around Enderly Park for a deadly jump shot and an impeccably executed pick and roll.

Name: Jeanie McGowan
Hometown: Buffalo, Missouri (Springfield, Missouri)
Current Home: Jefferson City, Missouri
College: University of Maryland (Verdun, France), Missouri Southern College-Joplin, and University of Missouri-Columbia
Seminary/Divinity School: Central Baptist Theological Seminary, 2003

Favorite Activities: Reading, movies, great conversation, being with my family, being active in social justice issues, spending time in New York City, and traveling in general

Interests: Music (violin, singing, listening), interior design, mentoring, cooking, historic preservation

About Me: I love learning and experiencing "aha!" moments in theology. I love equipping people and figuring out how to simplify my life in every way. Our recent move into a new, diverse neighborhood has been a wonderful experience with a new adventure every day! My life has been enriched by rubbing shoulders each day with people who struggle just to get by. I'm learning so much from them.

Name: Rick Bennett
Hometown: Live Oak, Florida
Current Home: Tampa, Florida
College: Florida State University, 1990
Seminary/Divinity School: Southwestern Baptist Theological Seminary, 1994
Blog: http://djword.blogspot.com

Favorite Activities: Reading and writing, exasperating my kids, avoiding hard work, hanging out with nonchurch people, attending cultural events (lowbrow and high), cooking when able and home brewing, trying to save the world.

Interests: Music (typical rock critic), film (film snob), the big three sports, philosophy, ethics, politics and advocacy, social justice issues, reading and writing, outside activities, travel, organic food, local food, foodie food, barbeque, environmental issues, saving the world

About Me: I am a son, husband, father of three kids with two middle names apiece, canine companion, and director of Spiritual Care for a Florida hospice organization (but I am not defined by my job). I am also a church planter, a business owner and a non-profit starter, and a failed novelist. I have worked in churches in Florida, Texas, Virginia, and Massachusetts. I helped start Ecclesia in Houston and planted an early emerging church in Boston focused on social justice and micro churches. I have worked for an organization helping homeless families and as a radio DJ and concert promoter. I am on the Coordinating Group for Emergent Village (which I have been involved in since its inception) and started cohorts in multiple cities.

Name: Zach Roberts
Hometown: Lynchburg, Virginia
Current Home: Raleigh, North Carolina
College: Bluefield College, 1996
Seminary/Divinity School: Southwestern Baptist Theological Seminary, 2000; Columbia Theological Seminary, 2010?
Blog: http://baptimergent.wordpress.com

Favorite Activities: Going to the pool with the family, going on "foodie" adventures with my wife, iTunes dance parties in the living room with the kids, smoking pork barbeque for a mess of friends, backpacking, reading, writing, enjoying craft beer, cigars on the porch, gaming, traveling, and watching *The Office.*

Interests: Neomonasticism, contemplative spirituality, postcolonial theology, green theology, church history, biblical history, re-imagining spiritual practices, parable writing, poetry, storytelling, pop culture

About Me: I am a husband, father, son, and friend. My wife's name is Jenn, and we have been married twelve years. We have two hilarious children—a daughter, Landyn, and a son, Harrison. Vocationally, I am a Jesus pilgrim who enjoys sharing various legs of the journey with fellow wanderers, mystics, heretics, and friends. You can find me trying to pull that off under the auspices of associate pastor for education at Ridge Road Baptist Church in Raleigh, North Carolina.

Name: Amy Canosa
Hometown: Mt. Airy, North Carolina
Current Home: Chapel Hill, North Carolina
College: Campbell University, 2003
Seminary/Divinity School: Duke Divinity School, 2008

Favorite Activities: Solving the world's problems, attending UNC-Chapel Hill sporting events, watching movies, reading, playing board/card games (especially Rook and Spades), cooking/baking for anyone and everyone that wants/needs food, listening to music, going to concerts, having deep and meaningful conversations.

Interests: Working with college students, social justice/peace-making issues and opportunities, poverty and hunger Issues, UNC basketball and football

About Me: I am the Cooperative Student Fellowship campus minister at the University of North Carolina at Chapel Hill. I also work as a chaplain resident at UNC Hospital in the trauma/surgical units. I love the beach, Taylor Swift songs, my dog Ellie, college students, anything Carolina Tarheel- related, the song "I'm Gonna Be (500 Miles)" by the Proclaimers, and the movie *Love Actually*. I love the Church and want to do everything I can to help bring about reconciliation in the world.

Name: Perry Lee Radford
Hometown: Rhodell, West Virginia
Current Residence: Bladensburg, Maryland
College: Washington Bible College, 1995
Seminary/Divinity School: Capital Bible Seminary
Blog: www.lstepministries.ning.com

Favorite Activities: Skiing, writing, producing and playing music with my Roland (Fantom X6 keyboard) and clarinet. I have been an avid roller-rink skater for about ten years and a portrait and landscape painter since I was nine years old.

Interests: My interests include exploring the countryside in the United States, particularly in West Virginia; discussing how to reach post-modern generations for Jesus; exploring the direction that today's church is headed in and where it should be headed; exploring musical sounds in worship that represent a departure from the traditional and popular contemporary gospel music; and in developing a missional congregation.

About Me: I am the third of four sons born to Deacon and Deaconness Nathaniel and Frances Radford. I was born in Mullens, West Virginia, and raised in Rhodell, West Virginia, which I still consider to be my home. I was baptized in Trinidad Baptist Church in Washington, D.C., at the age of sixteen under the late Rev. Daniel Jackson. I later joined Second Baptist Church Southwest, in southwest Washington, D.C. I announced my call to the gospel ministry in 1978 and began studying at the Washington Bible College. There I received an AA and BA in Pastoral Theology. I am working toward a master's degree at Capital Bible Seminary. A graduate of ITT Business Institute, I worked as a court and conference reporter and worked for the Department of Housing and Urban Development as a secretary for eight years before transferring to the World Bank where I have worked for twenty-two years as a program assistant and procurement assistant. Among the best things to ever happen to me are my relationship with Jesus Christ; my lovely wife, Betty; and my children. We're proud that our four children have done well; two have earned master's degrees, and two more are master's degree candidates.